Homeopathy
The Undiluted Facts

Edzard Ernst

Homeopathy
The Undiluted Facts

Including a Comprehensive A-Z Lexicon

 Springer

Edzard Ernst
Orford
UK

ISBN 978-3-319-43590-9   ISBN 978-3-319-43592-3   (eBook)
DOI 10.1007/978-3-319-43592-3

Library of Congress Control Number: 2016947397

Printed on acid-free paper

This Springer imprint is published by Springer Nature
The registered company is Springer International Publishing AG Switzerland

TO DANIELLE

Foreword

Since you are reading this foreword, I assume you have some interest in homeopathy. Hence, my task is to help you decide whether to read the rest of this book. Before proceeding though, you should know two things about me. First, much of my professional life has involved writing and teaching about "evidence-based medicine" and the better evaluation of treatments, particularly the use of controlled clinical trials. Second, I chaired the recent Australian NHMRC's review of the evidence on homeopathy referred to in this book. I now dearly wish I had had this book to read—it would have made a wonderful background and road map.

The book you have in your hands is written by the ideal author. Many texts on homeopathy or complementary medicines are polarized and biased—strongly for (by practitioners of homeopathy) or against (by scientists who have little or no experience of homeopathy). But Ernst is both and more. As he describes:

> As a youngster growing up in Germany, I was regularly treated by our family doctor who was a nationally famous homeopath. As a junior doctor I worked in a homeopathic hospital, practised homeopathy, and was impressed with its results.

Then later, as a professor of complementary medicine at the University of Exeter, he did many studies of homeopathy (as well as many other areas of medicine). I can't imagine a better background from which to write with experience and objectivity about homeopathy. An insightful and enjoyable example of his balanced discussions is the section in Chap. 10 on *Spurious Arguments by Proponents of Homeopathy*, followed by *Spurious Argument by Opponents of Homeopathy*. Both proponents and opponents would do well to read these eight pithy pages of wisdom.

It is worth looking at two of those arguments. Proponents argue that "only homeopaths understand homeopathy well enough," which Ernst points out as a perfect circular argument: We should only listen to expert homeopaths, but of course they do not doubt homeopathy or they would no longer practice. Ernst himself has practiced, which helps to overcome this (circular) objection. However, the opponents often say that "there is no credible evidence at all that supports homeopathy," but he points out that there are several well-conducted clinical studies of homeopathy which have had positive results. Indeed, the NHMRC review looked at 57 systematic reviews (on 68 medical conditions) which included 176 individual controlled trials and concluded from these that there "was no discernible convincing effects beyond placebo." But there were some "positive" studies: As might be expected from 176 trials, a few were "statistically significant" (p-value less 5 %, which is a 1 in 20 chance); however, just by chance 1/20 of 176 would mean about 9 which luck would class as "statistically significant." Untangling the complexities of such evidence requires solid knowledge of both research and homeopathy. And Ernst has both.

So who should read this book? I would suggest anyone wanting simple, factual, and reliable material on homeopathy and related issues. While it is written primarily for laypeople—and avoids jargon and taking sides—it is delightful and informative read for both laypeople and professionals in health care of all types. Read, enjoy, and be better informed.

May 2016   Paul Glasziou
Director, Centre for Research in Evidence-Based Practice
Bond University, Australia

Contents

Part I
The Facts of the Matter

Chapter 1
Introduction

Homeopathy has been with us for more than 200 years. During this time, it has come in and out of fashion, but finally it seems to have conquered the world. Today, homeopathy is not just popular in Europe, where it originated, it is also used widely in the USA, India, South America, and many other parts of the world. Millions of patients and consumers swear by homeopathy and employ its remedies on a daily basis.

Yet, despite this impressive success, homeopathy has remained one of the most controversial and divisive subjects in all of health care. Some people seem to believe in it with a quasi-religious fervour, while others loath it with a similarly deeply-felt passion. What is worse, the exchanges between the two camps are frequently emotional and less than tolerant. In this climate, it is far from easy for consumers to find simple, factual, and reliable material on this subject.

My book aims to fill this gap by providing clear and concise information about homeopathy and related issues. It is written primarily for laypeople who have an interest in health care and are perhaps tempted to try homeopathy for this or that ailment. I therefore avoid jargon and do my best to abstain from taking sides.

Most publications that have previously been written on this subject—and there are many of them—were, of course, authored by believers in homeopathy. Their stance is often regrettably uncritical or even overtly promotional. Many of these authors fail to disclose their *conflicts of interest* and make highly misleading, *biased* statements and therapeutic claims which potentially endanger the health of anyone who mistakes them for the truth. Consumers are clearly not best served by this type of approach.

A much smaller number of books has been authored by *critics of homeopathy*. They tend to be scathing not only about the therapy itself, but often also about its practitioners and users. Such books are frequently written by people who do not have a full understanding of the subject matter and sceptics who engage in what might be called 'homeopathy-bashing'. This approach is obviously not in the best interest of the consumer either.

© Springer International Publishing Switzerland 2016
E. Ernst, *Homeopathy - The Undiluted Facts*,
DOI 10.1007/978-3-319-43592-3_1

In order to provide responsible and reliable information, it would be helpful, perhaps even necessary, to have the following types of expertise:

- a sound knowledge of *evidence-based medicine*,
- the ability to tell good from poor *science*,
- *experience* as a patient who has been a patient treated by a homeopath,
- research experience in homeopathy,
- published *scientific* papers on the subject,
- application of homeopathy in clinical practice,
- skills of systematic analysis and *critical thinking*.

I can honestly say that I tick all these boxes and should thus be able to present the facts about homeopathy pure and simple.

As a youngster growing up in Germany, I was regularly treated by our family doctor who was a nationally famous *homeopath*. As a junior doctor I worked in a homeopathic hospital, practised homeopathy, and was impressed with its results. Later I researched homeopathy, published around 150 papers on the subject, frequently voicing concern about the quality of the *evidence*. Most importantly perhaps, I have no 'axe to grind': I am not—and never have been—in the pocket of the homeopathic industry, nor have I ever been on the payroll of 'Big Pharma'. All my professional life, I have been an independent academic physician answerable only to my peers, medical *ethics*, and *scientific* as well as professional standards.

With this book, I hope to analyse the known facts fairly and *critically* with a view to enabling my readers to make up their own minds. This book is based on the all-important principle that good medicine must demonstrably generate more good than harm. Where this is not the case, I will say so without attempting to hide the truth.

My foremost aim is to provide a service to consumers by reporting the *scientific* facts in an accessible way. Most people who are tempted to try homeopathy and even many users of homeopathy have little idea what this type of treatment is all about. They might believe that it is akin to *herbal medicine*, for instance. Or they may assume that homeopathy works like *vaccinations*. Or they may think that homeopathy is synonymous with *holistic* health care. Misconceptions of this sort can never be a good basis for therapeutic decisions. I aim not to perpetuate old myths, but rather to facilitate well-informed, *evidence*-based decisions.

In case you are already fully convinced that homeopathy is an *effective* and *safe* treatment for all ailments, if you believe that homeopathy is the victim of a conspiracy by the evil pharmaceutical industry, if you think that I want to stir you towards using dangerous chemical drugs, then this is probably not a good book for you. If, on the other hand, you are persuaded that everything about homeopathy is utter rubbish, that homeopathy has made no contribution to health care at all, that everyone who reports benefit after using homeopathy is a fraud, or that all consumers who are tempted to try homeopathy are stupid, then this book is not what you want either.

My book follows a very simple and clear structure. It has two main parts. Each of the 10 chapters in the first part deals with one particular aspect of homeopathy. They are written in such a way that they should be understandable without consulting any of the other chapters. Where additional information, explanations, definitions, etc., are deemed helpful, they are provided by the A–Z lexicon which forms the second part of the book. Throughout the book, words in italics can be found in the lexicon. It complements the first part with short paragraphs on specific themes, issues, and topics. The A–Z lexicon also covers subjects that are not mentioned in the first part and are meant to complement it. The lexicon can thus stand alone as a small dictionary in its own right. Together, the two parts of the book should generate a full and rounded picture of homeopathy.

Chapter 2
Definition and Main Principles of Homeopathy

Despite the current popularity of homeopathy, many people fail to understand what it really is. A UK survey, for instance, suggested that 40 % of the public thought homeopathy meant 'natural or *herbal medicine*'. This is not just misleading; it is, as we will see, quite simply incorrect. But how can we define homeopathy? As it turns out, a good *definition of homeopathy* is more difficult to provide than anticipated.

One might simply state that homeopathy is the school of medicine that was first developed by Samuel *Hahnemann* (1755–1843). However, this would tell us very little about the nature of homeopathy. My American Illustrated Medical Dictionary from 1927, a time when homeopathy was still fairly popular in the US, offers a much more practical definition:

> Homeopathy is a system of therapeutics founded by Samuel Christian Fredrich Hahnemann based on the following theories: first, the doctrine of signatures, namely, that diseases are curable by those drugs which produce effects on the body similar to the symptoms of the disease (similia similibus currantur); second, that the effects of drugs are increased by giving them in minute doses, which are to be obtained by carrying dilution or trituration to an extreme limit; third, the notion that most chronic diseases are only a manifestation of suppressed itch or psora.

A more recent and more authorative definition was published in the *International Dictionary of Homeopathy*: it states that homeopathy is

> [...] a therapeutic method using substances whose effects, when administered to healthy subjects, correspond to the manifestations of the disorder in the individual patient.

This sentence does describe homeopathy accurately, but it is perhaps too academic to be easily understood. It might be simpler to say that homeopathy is the use of homeopathic remedies for medicinal purposes. This, of course, would beg the question, what is a homeopathic remedy? The answer is easy, albeit not very enlightening; the International Dictionary of Homeopathy informs us that a homeopathic remedy is a

© Springer International Publishing Switzerland 2016
E. Ernst, *Homeopathy - The Undiluted Facts*,
DOI 10.1007/978-3-319-43592-3_2

medicinal agent which has been manufactured according to a method stipulated in a homeopathic *pharmacopoeia*. To explain this a bit better, it might be advisable to go gently, step by step.

Many people believe that homeopathic remedies are all based on plants and other natural substances. The truth, however, is that they can be made from almost any material; some are even based on immaterial sources such as *X-rays*. As many are made from plant extracts, and I will use plants as an example to explain briefly how homeopathic remedies are manufactured. More details on the various processes and phenomena involved in the manufacture of homeopathic preparations can be found in the following chapters and in the second part of this book (Fig. 2.1).

Homeopaths call the original plant extract for the production of a remedy a *mother tincture*. This name is fitting: the mother tincture can 'give birth' to a countless amount of further remedies. Most, but not all, homeopathic remedies are diluted several times—homeopaths speak of *serial dilution*—in a process called *potentisation* or *dynamisation*. This means that some homeopathic remedies (the ones that are not highly diluted) do contain plenty of material from the mother tincture, while many more are so highly diluted that they contain only a few molecules, and most homeopathic remedies are far too dilute to contain even a single molecule of the mother tincture. A C1 *potency*, for instance, is a 1:100 dilution of the mother tincture, while a C10 potency signifies a dilution of 1 part of mother tincture in 100 000 000 000 000 000 000 parts of *diluent*.

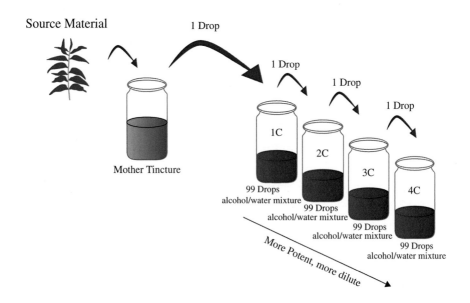

Source Material   1 Drop

Mother Tincture

1C

2C

3C

4C

1 Drop

1 Drop

1 Drop

99 Drops
alcohol/water mixture

99 Drops
alcohol/water mixture

99 Drops
alcohol/water mixture

99 Drops
alcohol/water mixture

More Potent, more dilute

Each vial is shaken vigorously after each dilution is made.

Fig. 2.1 Potentisation. This process involves serial dilutions with succussion at each step

If the plant extract in the mother tincture happens to be toxic—many substances used in homeopathy are very poisonous indeed—a C1 potency could easily generate quite serious side-effects. But normally, homeopathic remedies are sold in high potencies (C30 is probably the most popular potency and describes a dilution at the ratio of 1:1 000 000 000 000 000 000 000 000 000 000 000 000 000 000 000 000 000 000 000), which should be entirely free of side-effects, even if its mother tincture is as toxic as *arsenic*, which happens to be a popular homeopathic remedy.

What follows from all this is actually quite simple: most homeopathic remedies are given in high potencies which contain not enough molecules to cause harm. However, this does not mean that low potencies are necessarily harmless as well. In other words, the vast majority of homeopathic remedies cannot cause side-effects, but some undoubtedly have the potential to cause harm.

The practice of homeopathy is based on three unique and entirely independent assumptions—homeopaths like to think of them as *laws*—which were all developed by Samuel Hahnemann, homeopathy's founder.

2.1 Like Cures Like

Homeopathy is first and foremost based on the *like cures like principle* formulated by Hahnemann as 'simila similibus currentur' (strictly speaking this should not be translated as 'like cures like', but by the subjunctive 'let like be cured by like'). The principle—in fact, it is more an assumption than a principle—holds that, if a substance causes a set of symptoms in a healthy person, it can serve as a remedy for treating these symptoms when they occur in a patient. In the words of Hahnemann:

> Every medicine which [...] reproduces most of [the symptoms] present in a given disease, is capable of curing that disease.

Hahnemann called his discovery an 'eternal, universal *law* of nature.'

A few examples might explain the *law of similars*, as it is often called, better than long theoretical elaborations:

- A typical homeopathic treatment for hay fever would be a preparation of onion. Onions can make our eyes water, which is of course a symptom of hay fever.
- Coffee can keep us awake. A typical homeopathic remedy for insomnia is therefore based on coffee.
- A more exotic, but nevertheless real, example is the homeopathic remedy know as *Berlin wall*. The Berlin wall inhibited communication between people. For homeopaths, this is an indication that a remedy made from fragments of the original Berlin wall can cure a patient's communication problems.

The main problem here is that homeopaths see the like cures like principle as a true law of nature. Few people would deny that, under certain circumstances, a small dose of a substance that caused ill effects can reduce the harm. For instance, some people feel much improved when they drink a glass of beer after an alcoholic excess the night before. Like might cure like in very special situations, but it is not a law that is applicable to all substances and all situations.

Hahnemann developed some rather vague ideas as to how his remedies might bring about the clinical improvements which he thought he observed in his patients. Following his logic of like cures like, he believed that homeopathic remedies cause a set of symptoms, not just in healthy volunteers, but also in patients receiving homeopathic treatments. He called this an *artificial disease*, and postulated that this artificial disease would stimulate the patient's *vital force*, which would in turn defeat the patient's real disease. For this to happen, the artificial disease needed to be as similar as possible to the real disease affecting the patient.

2.2 Less Is More

As already mentioned, many mother tinctures used in homeopathy are toxic; examples include *arsenic*, lead, or strychnine. For homeopaths, poisonous substances do not necessarily present a problem, because they dilute their remedies multiple times (*serial dilution*). At each dilution step, they shake them vigorously. Homeopaths call this process of shaking a remedy *succussion*, and the process of serial dilution together with the shaking is called *potentisation* or *dynamisation*. As implied by the term 'potentisation', homeopaths are convinced that this unique method of preparing their remedies renders them not less but more potent. They speak of the *law of infinitesimals*.

Initially, the dilution was aimed purely at avoiding toxicity of the ingredient. Later, Hahnemann became convinced that the process transfers some information or *vital energy* from the less to the more dilute remedy. In this way, homeopaths believe, the diluent retains important properties of the mother tincture, even when all of this material has disappeared during serial dilutions, a phenomenon which is often referred to as the *memory of water*.

In Hahnemann's own words:

> [...] the power of a medicine in solution is much increased by intimate mixture with a large volume of fluid.

And elsewhere he stated that

> [...] as the smallest quantity of medicine naturally disturbs the organism least, we should choose the very smallest doses, provided always that they are a match for the disease [...] hardly any dose of the homeopathically selected remedy can be so small as not to be stronger than the natural disease.

Hahnemann came to believe that the healing power of his remedies did not depend on the substances contained in them, but that their "action must be called spirit-like".

2.3   Miasm Theory of Disease

The third main assumption of homeopathy is perhaps the most complex. It is also the one that many of today's homeopaths hesitate to believe in. It is the notion that all human diseases are caused by *miasms*, noxious vapours or atmospheres.

Hahnemann postulated the existence of three such entities: the *psoric*, sycotic, and syphilitic miasms. The most important miasm by far is the psora-miasm. In Hahnemann's opinion, psora was responsible for seven-eighths of all human diseases, while the venereal miasms, syphilis and sycosis, were the cause of all the remaining conditions:

> Psora is the sole true and fundamental cause that produces all the other countless forms of disease, which, under the names of nervous debility, hysteria, hypochondriasis, insanity, melancholy, idiocy, madness, epilepsy, and spasms of all kinds, softening of the bones, or rickets, scoliosis and cyphosis, caries, cancer, fungus haematodes, gout—yellow jaundice and cyanosis, dropsy—gastralgia, epistaxis, haemoptysis—asthma and suppuration of the lungs—megrim, deafness, cataract and amaurosis—paralysis, loss of sense, pains of every kind, etc., appear in our pathology as so many peculiar, distinct, and independent diseases.

Chronic diseases are, according to Hahnemann, the result of the invasion of the body by miasms through the skin. If left untreated or—much worse in Hahnemann's view—supressed by *allopathic* treatments, the miasms would spread throughout the body and cause chronic diseases. These conditions would often occur only years later. In order to prevent this course of events, many homeopaths employ anti-psoric remedies, the most important of which is sulphur.

Hahnemann interpreted miasm as an infection or a cloud full of illness-causing elements. In this way, Hahnemann might even have anticipated the *germ theory of disease* as well as important principles of immunity and disease prevention, all of which were formulated only well after his death. This seems particularly clear in Hahnemann's comments about cholera:

> On board of ships [...] the cholera miasm finds a favourable element for its multiplication, and grows into an enormously increased brood of those excessively minute, invisible, living creatures [...] of which the contagious matter of the cholera most probably consists [...] this concentrated aggravated miasm kills several of the crew; the others, however, being frequently exposed to the danger of infection [...] become fortified against it and no longer liable to be infected.

It has to be said, however, that Hahnemann's voluminous writings are by no means free of contradictions about many issues, and the subject of miasm is no exception: elsewhere he speaks of miasm as disease patterns which are not transmitted but inherited.

In addition to these three main assumptions, Hahnemann formulated numerous further rules and concepts he wanted his followers to adhere to. For instance, he believed that we cannot understand the nature of a disease. Therefore, disease is best described by the range of symptoms it produces. He also insisted that, in order not to jeopardise the success of homeopathic remedies, nothing should interfere with their actions.

This meant that patients were forbidden to ingest stimulants like coffee, spices, alcohol, or conventional medicines while taking homeopathic remedies. The latter point is particularly important, as it renders Hahnemann's homeopathy a truly *alternative medicine*, a therapy that replaces all others. Hahnemann was adamant that homeopathy was not to be combined with other forms of health care; he even called homeopaths who failed to obey to this rule 'traitors'.

Chapter 3
Myths About Homeopathy

In and around homeopathy, there seem to exist many more myths and misunderstandings than facts. The resulting confusion tends to mislead not only consumers but many health care professionals as well. If we want to make progress in this area, it is essential to debunk the myths, clear up the misunderstandings, and start disseminating reliable information.

This short chapter is an attempt to highlight some of the most important misconceptions and half-truths (in no particular order and as concisely as possible) and to contrast them with equally brief statements describing the generally accepted truths. The purpose of this exercise is to challenge widespread opinions and alert the reader's mind to the issues to be covered in the following chapters. The rest of the book will discuss them more fully by providing the necessary background, facts, and details. Finally, Chap. 10 will go 'full circle' by revisiting some of the myths mentioned here and offering reminders of the most relevant themes, arguments, and counter-arguments.

Homeopathic remedies are natural. Arguably there is nothing natural about the way homeopathic preparations are *potentised*, and some remedies are unquestionably manufactured of man-made *stock*, e.g., *Berlin Wall*.

Homeopathy is entirely devoid of risks. When highly *dilute*, homeopathic remedies have no side-effects, but if people use homeopathy instead of a conventional therapy for serious conditions, they may put their health at *risk*.

Homeopathy is similar to herbal medicine. *Herbal* medicine exclusively employs plant extracts which are neither potentised nor used according to the *like cures like* principle. Homeopaths employ all types of substances which are then potentised and used under the like cures like principle.

Homeopathy is holistic. All good medicine is *holistic*, and homeopathy, as practised today, is not more holistic than other forms of health care.

© Springer International Publishing Switzerland 2016
E. Ernst, *Homeopathy - The Undiluted Facts*,
DOI 10.1007/978-3-319-43592-3_3

All homeopathic remedies are highly diluted. Most have indeed undergone *serial dilution*, but some are not highly diluted and can, in fact, contain considerable amounts of active ingredients.

Homeopathic remedies can never cause serious side-effects. Homeopathic *arsenic* in the D1 *potency*, for instance, contains sufficient amounts of arsenic to cause toxic effects.

Homeopaths are all medical doctors. Some *homeopaths* have studied medicine, but the majority are lay or professional homeopaths who have not been to medical school.

Homeopaths have no medical training. Those who have been to medical school clearly do have medical training. Some *lay homeopaths* have years of education and training, while others may have little or no training. The requirements for being allowed to call yourself a homeopath vary hugely from country to country.

Homeopaths treat the root causes of an illness. From a homeopathic perspective, this statement may seem to be correct; from a scientific or medical perspective, however, it is misleading. A homeopath may claim that the root cause of an illness is a disturbance in the *vital force*, while conventional clinicians would see such an assumption as obsolete and argue that each disease has *specific* causes which have to be addressed whenever possible.

Homeopathy is always highly individualized. The prescriptions in *classical homeopathy* are indeed tailor-made for each patient. But there are other forms of homeopathy, for instance *clinical homeopathy*, where prescriptions are not based on the individual characteristics of the patient but on the condition he or she is suffering from, much like in conventional medicine.

Homeopathy can only work if a homeopath has determined the ideal remedy based on a long consultation. True, classical homeopaths might say that; but the reality is that homeopathic remedies are currently for sale in many outlets, and many consumers take them without any consultation whatsoever.

Homeopathy must not be combined with conventional treatments. *Hahnemann*, the father of homeopathy, was very much against mixing homeopathy with anything else. Today, however, few homeopaths heed his advice.

All homeopathic treatments are for oral consumption. Most are indeed to be taken by mouth, but some are for external use or even for injecting into the body.

Homeopathic remedies are cheap. Very high *potencies* have to be diluted and *succussed* many times, and this process can make the end-product expensive.

Homeopaths will treat any disease. Some *homeopaths* do, but most would recommend seeing a conventional practitioner in cases of serious illness.

Homeopathic remedies cannot be placebos because they work for children. This argument is based on poor logic: even small children can respond to *placebos*.

There are several plausible explanations as to the *mechanism of action* **of homeopathic remedies.** Currently, there are several *theories* about the mode of action, but none of them has been generally accepted outside the realm of homeopathy.

There is a worldwide conspiracy against homeopathy. So far, nobody was able to produce any evidence for the widespread assumption of a *conspiracy*.

The homeopathic industry is fundamentally different from 'Big Pharma'. The homeopathic industry is much smaller than the *pharmaceutical industry*. However, their behavior is in many respects not significantly different: both aim to make a profit and both occasionally 'sail close to the wind' in order to reach this aim.

Homeopathy cannot be tested in scientific trials. Many *scientific* studies have been published which have allowed for *individualization* and all the other requirements of homeopathy.

There is not a single positive trial of homeopathy. Some sceptics claim this to be true, but it is false. There are many studies that have suggested homeopathic remedies to be better than placebo.

Homeopathic remedies work like vaccines. Contrary to most highly *diluted* remedies, *vaccines* do contain measurable amounts of active ingredients and they cause measurable responses of the immune system.

Conventional doctors treat the disease, homeopaths treat the patient. "The good physician treats the disease; the great physician treats the patient who has the disease", stated William Osler, and he was, of course, correct: all good medicine is patient-centred.

Chapter 4
Current Popularity, Acceptance, and Regulation of Homeopathy

Considering the atrocious risks of *heroic medicine*—the name given retrospectively to the conventional treatments of Hahnemann's time—it is easy to see why homeopathy quickly conquered the world. Partly stimulated by *Hahnemann's* criticism, conventional medicine gradually began to abandon its dangerous treatments and became more and more *scientific*. Consequently, it began to discover ever more *effective* treatments. These developments significantly contributed to a decline in homeopathy's popularity during the late 19th and early 20th centuries. The downturn only changed in the 1970s when *alternative medicine*—and with it homeopathy—started to experience a revival. Today homeopathy has again a sizeable following, particularly in Germany, France, India, Britain, and the US.

In Germany, Hahnemann's homeland, homeopathy has never been entirely out of favour. In 1970, an estimated 24 % of German consumers used homeopathy. By 2009, this figure had risen to 57 % and, in 2013, it had reached a staggering 60 %. About 50 % of all German general practitioners are said to employ homeopathy at least occasionally. The conditions they treat most frequently with homeopathy include common colds, *flu*, insect bites, sunburns, headaches, gastrointestinal problems, and sleeplessness. A total of 26 % of the drugs used for German children are alternative medicines, and 53.7 % of those are homeopathic remedies. About 15 000 *Heilpraktiker*, non-medically trained health practitioners practising all types of alternative therapies, are registered in Germany and the majority of them employ homeopathy in their daily practice.

In France, over 6.7 million patients—about 10 % of the population—receive at least one reimbursement for a homeopathic preparation per year. The annual cost of all prescribed homeopathic treatments is approximately €279 million, which equates to 0.3 % of France's total drug bill. About 44 % of all French health care professionals (nearly 95 % of general practitioners, dermatologists, and paediatricians, and 75 % of midwives) prescribe homeopathic remedies. Homeopathy accounts for 5 % of the total number of drugs prescribed in France.

In the UK, homeopathy has enjoyed royal protection ever since it was first introduced in the 19th century. In particular, *Prince Charles* is an outspoken advocate of homeopathy who has been known to lobby politicians in its cause. Until recently,

© Springer International Publishing Switzerland 2016
E. Ernst, *Homeopathy - The Undiluted Facts*,
DOI 10.1007/978-3-319-43592-3_4

there were 5 homeopathic *NHS* hospitals. Today, only two of them survive, and even they have changed their names, omitting the word 'homeopathy' from it. About 10 % of British general practitioners treat patients with homeopathic remedies. Referral rates by general practitioners to homeopaths vary from 5 to 73 % according to locality. On average 15 % of general practitioners endorse homeopathy, and less than 10 % use it for themselves. The over-the-counter sales of homeopathics stood, according to a Mintel report of 2012, at around £ 46 million. However, the *expenditure* of the NHS on homeopathy has declined sharply during the last decade (Fig. 4.1).

In the European Union as a whole, homeopathy is said to be the most popular form of *alternative medicine*. An estimated 45 000 medical and 5 800 non-medical clinicians practise homeopathy in the region. The annual sales of homeopathic remedies in Europe now exceed one billion Euros. About 90 % of this expenditure comes from France, followed by Germany, Netherlands, Spain, Belgium, the UK, and Poland.

In the USA, the use of homeopathy has increased steadily, after a sharp decline during the early years of the 20th century. Around 10 million Americans currently use homeopathics every year, and 30 homeopathic schools train *homeopaths*. The sales of homeopathic remedies reached US$ 3 billion in 2008, a figure which is still growing steadily as the average out-of-pocket cost of accessing standard medical care rises, encouraging more people to turn to self-medication instead of using physician services. The annual expenditure for visits to homeopaths in the USA is around US$ 170 million. In 1997, 17 % of US citizens had consulted a homeopath in the last 12 months. Many chiropractors and *naturopaths* also use homeopathy. Between 19 and 29 % of US naturopaths, for instance, employ homeopathy regularly.

Fig. 4.1 Queen Elizabeth has a long-standing interest in homeopathy and expressed the wish to meet Professor Ernst shortly after he was appointed in 1993 to the first chair in complementary medicine at Exeter University

In India, the popularity of homeopathy has grown steadily since it was introduced in the 18th century. In 1973, the Indian government officially recognised homeopathy and set up the Central Council of Homeopathy to regulate its practice. Today, over 200 000 homeopaths work in India, and homeopathy is the third most popular form of health care in this country, after conventional medicine and Ayurveda. However, the Indian National Sample Survey Office recently suggested that only 6 % of the Indian population trusted what the investigators (erroneously) called 'Indian systems of medicine', e.g., Ayurveda, Unani, and Siddha, homeopathy, yoga, and naturopathy.

Across the globe, the popularity of homeopathy differs considerably from country to country. One *systematic review* suggested that the usage rates for homeopathy are currently highest in Germany, followed by the UK, and Canada, ranging from 1 to 39 % with a global average of 11 %. However, only around 1.5 % of all consumers are said to consult homeopaths. The popularity of homeopathy is also reflected in sales figures of homeopathic remedies: *Boiron*, the world's largest manufacturer of homeopathic remedies with bases in many countries worldwide, reported half-year sales of over € 275 000 000 in 2015.

The legal recognition and *regulation* of homeopathy show considerable national variations. Furthermore, they are, of course, changing over time. In some parts of the world, e.g., southern Europe and Austria, only doctors, *veterinary* surgeons, and *dentists* are allowed to practise homeopathy. Elsewhere, e.g., in Sweden and Slovenia, doctors could be struck off the medical register, if they did. In Germany and Austria, a doctor can obtain additional qualifications in homeopathy by undertaking officially recognised courses. In other countries, e.g., Belgium and India, homeopathy is even an officially recognised medical specialty. In the UK, *medical homeopaths* exist side by side with *lay homeopaths* who have no mandatory training in medicine. In some regions of the US, lay-homeopaths face medical practice acts, which prohibit the unlicensed practice of medicine, as well as scope of practice limitations, which restrict what non-medical providers are allowed to diagnose and treat.

Veterinary homeopathy is recognised and regulated by many governments. In the EU, for instance, about 2 000 veterinary surgeons ($\sim$1 % of the total) provide homeopathic treatments for *animals*. By contrast, in Sweden, vets are not allowed to practise homeopathy. In the UK, Prince Charles is a prominent advocate of veterinary homeopathy. In 2005, he wrote:

> One of the big arguments used against homeopathy is that it does not really work medically. The criticism is that people simply believe they are going to feel better and so they think they are better. They have responded to the so-called 'placebo effect'. It is for this reason that critics of homeopathy argue that it is a trick of the mind and its remedies are nothing more than sugar pills. What none of those who take this view ever seem to acknowledge is that these remedies also work on animals, which are surely unlikely to be influenced by the placebo effect. I certainly remember that when I started to introduce homeopathic remedies on the Duchy Home Farm, farm staff who had no view either way reported that the health of an animal that had been treated had improved so I wonder what it is that prevents the medical profession from even considering the evidence that now exists of trials of homeopathic treatments carried out on animals? It is not the quackery they claim it to be. Or if it is, then I have some very clever cows in my shed!

In several countries, e.g., Germany, Poland, and Spain, homeopathy is being taught at university level. Elsewhere tuition for homeopaths is provided in private institutions. In most countries, homeopathic treatments are reimbursed by the public or private health insurance systems.

Much of the information in this chapter is based on surveys, and it should be pointed out that most of such investigations are less than rigorous. Thus they can—and often do—produce information which is either not reliable or is outright misleading. Despite this important caveat, it seems fair to conclude from the large volume of data available to date that, despite the obvious variations over time and the inevitable differences between countries, homeopathy is currently used by many patients worldwide. Homeopaths tend to argue that any treatment that is appreciated by millions must be *safe* and *effective*. As we will see in the following chapters, this is little more than a *fallacy*.

More detailed information on the regulation of homeopathy in the EU is available via the CAMbrella website (http://cambrella.eu/home.php?il=203&l=deu).

Chapter 5
History of Homeopathy

When discussing the history of homeopathy, it is unavoidable to consider the life of its founder, Christian Friedrich Samuel *Hahnemann* (1755–1843). As many excellent biographies of Hahnemann already exist, I do not feel the need to review his fascinating life in full detail here. Instead I will merely focus on those events and aspects that seem relevant to the understanding of homeopathy.

5.1 The Life of Hahnemann

Hahnemann was born in 1755 in Meissen, where his father was employed as a porcelain painter in the famous local porcelain factory. Despite being poor, his parents secured him an excellent education; even at an early age, Hahnemann spoke several languages. Later he was able to finance his medical studies in Leipzig, *Vienna*, and Erlangen. He remained in Erlangen for only four months, but managed to submit a MD thesis to receive his doctorate in 1779. In a rare display of humility, he stated about his thesis:

> I will frankly admit that the short time I had to prepare this dissertation was only enough to draw a sketch. It is to be hoped that in the future a more erudite and experienced person will use this disordered and raw material for a more systematic and complete approach.

Subsequently, he wrote three further theses at different universities. The second two theses of 1784 dealt with obstetrical matters; one was a precondition for becoming a medical officer in Wittenberg, a position he wanted for mainly financial reasons. His fourth thesis of 1812 at the University of Leipzig was a dissertation on a toxic plant, white hellebore; this in turn was a precondition for his being allowed to lecture at Leipzig university.

Hahnemann grew up to be a deeply religious and spiritual man as well as an eccentric, innovator, maverick, and polymath. Anthony Campbell, former consultant

© Springer International Publishing Switzerland 2016
E. Ernst, *Homeopathy - The Undiluted Facts*,
DOI 10.1007/978-3-319-43592-3_5

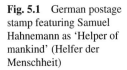

Fig. 5.1 German postage stamp featuring Samuel Hahnemann as 'Helper of mankind' (Helfer der Menschheit)

at the *Royal London Homeopathic Hospital*, put it succinctly: "Hahnemann believed himself to be God's chosen instrument for the healing of mankind".

In 1782, Hahnemann married the daughter of a *pharmacist* (he quarrelled with pharmacists throughout his life). The young couple's early years of married life were more than a little restless; between 1789 and 1805, their fast-growing family lived in dozens of different towns throughout eastern Germany (Fig. 5.1).

As a young physician, Hahnemann began to realise that the health care of his time was neither *safe* nor *effective*. Having gained this crucial insight, he became deeply disenchanted with the *heroic medicine* (see below) of his age, so much so that, for several years, he completely stopped practising as a clinician and tried to earn a living by translating medical texts.

In the course of this work, in 1790, he came across an explanation by the famous Scottish physician William Cullen (1710–1790) as to why *Cinchona* bark, an accepted cure for *malaria*, was effective. Hahnemann disagreed with Cullen's explanation that it worked as a tonic and decided to do some experiments of his own. His investigations essentially consisted in repeatedly taking large doses of Cinchona bark powder, which we know today to contain quinine, and carefully noting the effects upon his body. This experiment was, in fact, the very first homeopathic *proving*, a method of testing medicinal substances on healthy individuals.

What Hahnemann believed to have noticed in these *quinine experiments* determined the rest of his life and formed the very basis of homeopathy: this well-known malaria drug actually caused the symptoms of malaria when taken by a healthy individual. He eventually concluded that "Cinchona bark [...] acts because it can produce similar symptoms to those of intermittent fever [malaria] in healthy people".

Hahnemann tirelessly conducted more research on himself, family members, and friends, testing several other medicines in a similar fashion. Over and over again, he believed he noticed that a drug given to a healthy person would cause symptoms similar to the ones it cured in sick patients. After years of obsessively studying this phenomenon, he concluded that he had discovered a general *law* of nature: simila similibus currentur or the *like cures like* principle. It is neither a law nor a principle, but an assumption or theory; nevertheless, it was to become the fundament of an entirely new school of medicine. Hahnemann was an outspoken but by no means modest man: many years later, in a speech given in Paris towards the end of his long life, he called his discovery a "sublime revelation of an eternal law".

There are, of course, several historical precedents for this like cures like principle, and it is possible that Hahnemann, who was very well-read, had been aware of them. For instance, Hippocrates wrote: "By similar things a disease is produced and through the application of the like, it is cured." And Paracelsus stated: "Sames must be cured by sames." Yet it was undoubtedly Hahnemann who first investigated this theory systematically, formulated it, declared it to be a law of nature, and made it the central tenet of his new method, homeopathy. Hahnemann was convinced that his concepts were based on scientific inquiry and empirical proof; yet it is easy to see that they were also rooted in metaphysical theories and alchemic ideas of a 'mystical empiricist' (Fig. 5.2).

When Hahnemann finally felt confident about it, he published his revolutionary theory—his first article on the subject appeared in 1796, while the first edition of his major text, the *Organon*, was published in 1810. In order to gain clinical experience with his new therapeutic approach, Hahnemann returned to clinical practice. Subsequently, he added new ideas to his original concepts and almost constantly revised the Organon, which saw a total of six editions. Most notably, he began to use smaller and smaller doses—that is higher and higher *potencies*—of his remedies (Fig. 5.3).

Initially, Hahnemann did so mainly because he needed to minimise the side-effects of the frequently toxic substances he employed as medicines. In the 1820s, he thought he noticed the paradoxical phenomenon that *serial dilution* combined with *succussion* would render his remedies, not weaker, but stronger. He called his unique process of dilution and shaking his remedies *potentisation* or *dynamisation*, and became convinced that it was capable of awakening the healing powers even of otherwise inert substances such as plain table salt.

According to Hahnemann's theory, the administration of a homeopathic remedy would cause a set of symptoms which he called an *artificial disease*. This, he thought, would happen not just during *provings* in healthy volunteers, but also in patients. The only difference is, he thought, that in patients this would be less noticeable; it would just manifest itself as a slight worsening of their symptoms which he called a homeopathic *aggravation*. The artificial disease would somehow overcome the original disease of a patient and thus bring about the cure. He expressed this as follows:

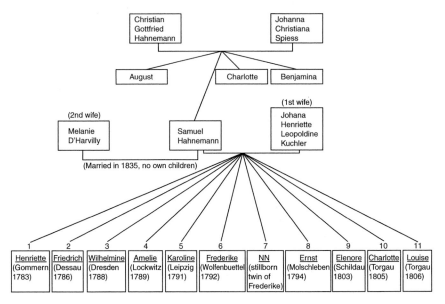

Fig. 5.2 Hahnemann family tree. Places and dates of birth are in brackets. Several of Hahnemann's children had remarkable lives. Friedrich became a homeopath and went mad, according to his father. He moved to Holland, England, Ireland, and finally America, where he vanished without a trace. Amalie had a son who, under the name Suess–Hahnemann, also became a homeopath. He lived in England and was one of Melanie's most outspoken critics. Ernst died before his first birthday after a fall from a carriage. Frederike was robbed and murdered in 1792 close to her home. Elenore published a book entitled Homeopathic Adviser for the Home, which her father called "a miserable patchwork". She was murdered and found dead in a pond in Koethen. After Hahnemann had married Melanie and moved with her to Paris, he left Charlotte and Louise who had until then looked after their elderly father in Koethen, where they both remained until their deaths

> The great homeopathic Law of Cures rests on this law of man's nature, revealed by experience, that diseases are only destroyed and cured by similar diseases.

Of note in this quote is the word 'only': Hahnemann was certain that his newly discovered approach was not just one treatment amongst several, but that it was the only one that could permanently heal patients.

If chosen correctly, this artificial disease closely resembled the disease of the patient and would, according to Hahnemann, stimulate the *vital forces* of the patient to eliminate the disease. For that to happen, the dose did not need to be substantial; in fact, *higher potencies* were more potent than low ones. In Hahnemann's words:

> If dilution is also employed (whereby the dose gains a greater power of expansion), an excessive effect is easily produced.

Hahnemann did not see a problem in the fact that tiny doses should have large effects, because he did not believe that his remedies depended on the material substance administered; the action of a homeopathic remedy, he concluded, "must be called spirit-like".

Fig. 5.3 Title page of
Hahnemann's Organon,
published in 1810. The full
title was Organon of the
Rational Healing Art
(Organon der rationellen
Heilkunde)

O r g a n o n

der rationellen

H e i l k u n d e

von

Samuel Hahnemann.

Die Wahrheit, die wir alle nöthig haben,
die uns als Menschen glücklich macht,
wird von der weisen Hand, die sie uns zugedacht,
nur leicht verdeckt, nicht tief vergraben.
GELLERT.

Dresden, 1810.
in der Arnoldischen Buchhandlung.

Even though Hahnemann's most voluminous writings are full of contradictions, it seems clear that he conceived homeopathic remedies, not as material drugs comparable to those of *allopathic* medicine, but as the "vital force captured in a bottle", as Anthony Campbell once put it. It is equally clear that he considered homeopathy, not as a complementary therapy, but as the only true medicine. He was most intolerant of those homeopaths—he called them 'half-homeopaths'—who combined homeopathy with other interventions:

> He who does not walk exactly the same line with me, who diverges, if it be the breadth of a straw, to the right or the left, is an apostate and a traitor and I will have nothing to do with him.

Patients generally approved of Hahnemann's new method, and it is not difficult to see why: in sharp contrast to the *heroic treatments* of his conventional colleagues, his remedies were free of side-effects. Hahnemann soon became famous and relatively affluent; finally, the financial worries that had been unwelcome companions all his life became a thing of the past. His colleagues, however, were not impressed; after all, his ideas were not just revolutionary, counter-intuitive and implausible, they also threatened their livelihoods. With few exceptions, the physicians of the time either ignored, condemned, defamed, or mocked homeopathy and its founder. For short periods of time, the practice of homeopathy was even forbidden in some countries, e.g., Austria and Russia.

Pharmacists fought homeopathy with even more fervour. Homeopaths insisted on producing their own medicines, and this did, of course, endanger the pharmacists' income. In 1820, they took Hahnemann to court for 'entrenching on their privileges' and virtually drove him out of Leipzig where he lived at the time. Throughout his life Hahnemann reacted to this type of challenge with counter-attacks, polemics, and a remarkable lack of diplomacy.

In 1821, Hahnemann settled in Koethen where, in 1830, after 48 years of marriage and 11 children, his wife died. At the time Hahnemann was 75, and his professional career appeared to be all but over. He seemed ready to settle down to a well-deserved retirement. Yet, only months later, he was to embark on to an entirely new adventure.

In October 1834, an exotic and attractive young female visitor came to consult him in Koethen. Melanie d'Hervilly had travelled all the way from Paris. The woman in her mid-30s came as a patient. Three months later the two were married, and three months later again they had moved to Paris. The sizeable Parisian homeopathic scene welcomed Samuel and *Melanie Hahnemann* with enthusiasm, and the couple was quickly able to establish a very successful and highly fashionable practice.

At this stage, Hahnemann had taken his idea of potentisation to new extremes. He postulated that the simple smell from an open remedy bottle could be therapeutic. *Olefaction* was a method of administrating homeopathic remedies that he had first considered in 1829, but subsequently abandoned. Sometimes he also advised some of his patients to use his remedies "for external rubbing".

Even though she had no medical background, Melanie had soon learned homeopathy from her husband and assisted him wherever she could. For the first time in his life, Hahnemann, who was now in his 80s, enjoyed happiness, fame and luxury. He continued writing, and worked on the sixth edition of his Organon until shortly before his death on 2 July 1848.

Apart from having invented and popularised homeopathy, Hahnemann has numerous other achievements to his name:

- He warned of the dangers of *heroic medicine*, and his warnings helped to generate significant improvements in conventional medicine.
- He was one of the first to systematically test the effects of drugs on healthy individuals (*provings*).
- He translated many important medical texts.
- He published innovative concepts about novel approaches for dealing with epidemics.
- He promoted environmental measures and life-style changes emphasising disease *prevention*.
- His *miasma* theory can be seen as anticipating the germ theory of disease.
- His concepts of treating mental disease were significantly ahead of his time.

- He made important contributions to chemistry.
- He argued against poly-pharmacy, the use of multiple medicines for the same condition.
- He stimulated rigorous research using methodologies such as *placebo*-controlled trials.
- He realised the importance of long, empathetic consultations.
- He realised the importance of practising according to *holistic* principles.
- He helped to make health care professions accessible to women.

Several authors have commented on Hahnemann's remarkable personality. The pro-homeopathic psychiatrist Jonathan Davidson offers the following diagnoses:

> There are reasons to suspect that Hahnemann had either a variant of bipolar disorder or at least a personality characterised by unusual levels of grandiosity, paranoia, abrasiveness, confrontational behaviour, and interpersonal sensitivity, flavoured with mood swings and a degree of misrepresentation, even dishonesty.

The homeopath William Wesselhoeft, who had studied under Hahnemann described his master as

> [...] an extreme fundamentalist in his beliefs in his own doctrines. He was as extravagant in his speculative claims as our evangelists, as vindictive as a politician the day before election, and as inconsistent as most human beings who persuade themselves that, because they know a lot about one thing, their opinions on other matters are invaluable and final.

Most biographers have pointed out that there is evidence of instability in Hahnemann's family: his son *Friedrich* seemed to have gone insane before he eventually disappeared without trace in America. Two of Hahnemann's daughters developed 'morbid anxiety', and two other daughters were murdered under strange circumstances.

5.2 Heroic Medicine

In Hahnemann's day, medicine relied largely on Galen's doctrine of the 'four humours'. Simply put, it assumed that health was determined by the correct balance of four bodily fluids; if an imbalance occurred, ill health would ensue. Treatment consisted of interventions aimed at re-establishing the balance (Fig. 5.4).

The main therapeutic method for achieving this was blood-letting. Several other therapies were available as well, e.g., leeches, blistering, intestinal purging, vomiting, profuse sweating, and toxic drugs like mercury. They might have been well-intentioned, but they were neither effective nor safe. In fact, heroic medicine was often more dangerous than the diseases it was supposed to treat.

Hahnemann's arguably greatest achievement was to realise that patients were ill-served by this type of health care. Once this fact had become clear to him, it would have been irresponsible to ignore it. Consequently, he stopped working as a clinician, regardless of the often extreme hardship this decision incurred on his growing family.

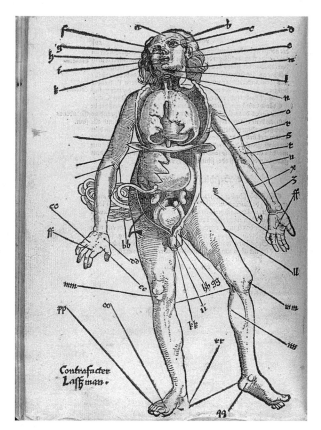

Fig. 5.4   Blood-letting. Hans von Gersdorff (surgeon) (ca. 1455–1529), Feldtbüch der Wundartzney (Strasbourg, 1519) Aderlasspunkte (Field book of surgery, Strasbourg 1519)

It is conceivable that these circumstances enforced his desire and need to innovate and find a form of treatment that would generate more good than harm.

Hahnemann was outspoken and rarely minced his words. About the medicine of his time, which he called *allopathy* and 'school medicine', he stated:

> Blood-letting, fever remedies […] and everlasting aperients and clysters form the circle in which the ordinary German physician turns round unceasingly.

Elsewhere he wrote:

> Of all therapies ever conceived there is none more allopathic, senseless and futile than Broussais' debilitating bloodletting and starvation diet, which have been widespread for years. No sensible man could ever find any medical benefit in such treatment, whereas a real medical substance, even arbitrarily chosen, has now and then helped a patient because it happened to be homeopathic. But what can common sense expect from bloodletting other than the certain impairment and shortening of life?

And about his allopathic colleagues he wrote:

> They seem to prefer delivering over all mankind the grave-digger, to listening to the good council of the new, purified healing art.

The inadequacies of heroic medicine undoubtedly contributed significantly to the early success of homeopathy. This was perhaps nowhere more obvious than with the encouraging results obtained with homeopathic treatment during major epidemics. Several comparisons between the conventional and the homeopathic approaches indicated that significantly more patients survived when treated homeopathically. Naturally, this was interpreted by homeopaths as the direct result of the homeopathic remedies administered. Whether this conclusion is correct, is more than doubtful. It ignores two important facts. Firstly, heroic medicine was actively harming patients, and even a *placebo* therapy would, in comparison, have been better. Secondly, homeopaths implemented hygienic and environmental measures in the treatment of epidemics which were well ahead of their time and which would have had a positive influence on the survival rates, unrelated to homeopathy itself.

5.3 International Success and Early Homeopaths

After the publication of Hahnemann's Organon, homeopathy soon attracted several active and enthusiastic followers. Some of these men took the new ideas to other countries, often with missionary zeal.

Hans Gram (1786–1840), a Danish homeopath, started practising in New York in 1825. However, it was Constantine Hering (1800–1880) who popularised homeopathy in the US in a much more decisive way. As a medical student in Germany, Hering had been given the task of writing a rebuttal of Hahnemann's concepts. However, in the course of this research, he became a convinced homeopath. In 1833, Hering settled in Philadelphia and, in 1844, he became the first president of the newly founded American Institute of Homeopathy. Homeopathy soon became more popular in the US than anywhere else in the world. Today, Hering is best known to homeopaths around the world for what is often called Hering's law, which postulates that the healing process frequently follows a typical pattern: symptoms improve from the head down, from inside out, from the most to the least important organs, and in reverse order of their appearance. He is also credited with helping to introduce both nitroglycerine and snake venoms into our therapeutic repertoire.

Only a few decades after homeopathy had arrived in America, the US had over 20 homeopathic colleges and around 60 homeopathic hospitals. The decline started in the late 19th century and was mainly due to three factors: conventional medicine was beginning to discover more and more effective treatments; endless in-fighting was dividing US homeopathy often to the point of destruction; and the US government abolished many homeopathic colleges which were perceived to be mere 'diploma mills' (Fig. 5.5).

Fig. 5.5   James Tyler Kent
(1849–1916)

James Tyler *Kent* (1849–1916) was converted from eclectic medicine to homeopathy when his first wife experienced a dramatic cure from a life-threatening condition after consulting a homeopath. After converting to homeopathy, Kent took the US homeopathy scene by storm. He is best known for his repertory which became so widely accepted that it is often referred to as *the repertory*. Kent adopted Hahnemann's later ideas and felt that they corresponded perfectly to the metaphysical teachings of *Swedenborg*. Kent believed that "homeopathy is founded on a divine order and that disease results from transgression of this order", as Anthony Campbell once put it. Kent was responsible for popularising *ultra-high potencies* and for dramatizing *drug pictures*, a concept originally introduced by Hering to make it easier to remember the effects of homeopathic remedies. According to Kent, the homeopathic remedy 'sepia', for example, "is suited to tall, slim women with narrow pelvis and lax fibres and muscles". This approach paved the way to *constitutional prescribing* and soon became highly prevalent also outside the US. Thus Kent's influence in homeopathy is second only to Hahnemann's (Fig. 5.6).

Fig. 5.6 Senate portrait of
Royal S. Copeland
(1868–1938)

Royal Copeland (1868–1938) qualified as a homeopath at the University of Michigan and later became an ophthalmic surgeon and prominent advocate of public health. Between 1908 and 1918, he served as dean at the New York Homeopathic and Flower Hospital College. During World War 1, he established the first wartime army homeopathic hospital, a considerable achievement, as homeopathy had been excluded from the military since the Civil War. His particular importance for US homeopathy, however, lies in the fact that he served for many years as a US senator and thus exerted considerable political influence. He was responsible for the Food, Drug, and Cosmetics Act of 1938 which protected homeopathy by including the Homeopathic *Pharmacopeia* of the United States as the legally binding standard that it still is today (Fig. 5.7).

Frederic Hervey Foster Quin introduced homeopathy to the UK. As a young physician, he had visited Hahnemann in Koethen in 1826. By 1832, Quin was fully converted to homeopathy and returned to England. Being well-connected to the European aristocracy, he managed to attract many influential personalities to homeopathy. In 1844, he founded the British Homeopathic Society and, in 1850, he opened the predecessor of the *Royal London Homeopathic Hospital*. The London Cholera

Fig. 5.7 Frederic Hervey
Foster Quin (1799–1878),
the first homeopathic
physician in England

epidemic of 1854 became a crucial event for this institution and arguably for homeopathy worldwide. This hospital's death rates were significantly lower than those of conventional hospitals. Similar results were also reported from other countries (see above).

Homeopathy was first introduced to India by a German doctor from Siebenbuergen, Johann Martin Honigberger (1795–1869). He first came to India in 1829 as a conventionally trained physician and treated, amongst other personalities, the Maharaja Ranjit Singh of Punjab. In 1834, he returned to Europe, met Hahnemann, and became a convert to homeopathy. Subsequently, he returned to India in 1839 and brought homeopathy to this country. Initially, homeopathy was practised mainly by *lay* practitioners because, under British rule, Indian citizens were not allowed to study medicine. Mahendra Lal Sircar was the first Indian to become a homeopathic physician, and he is often called the Hering of India. The Calcutta Homeopathic Medical College was established in 1881 and assumed a crucial role in popularising homeopathy (Fig. 5.8).

In general, the fate of homeopathy can be characterised by its ups and downs. A good and relatively well-researched example of this roller-coaster is the history of homeopathy in Hungary:

Fig. 5.8 Johann Martin
Honigberger (1795–1869)

- From 1819 onwards, homeopathy had been banned by the authorities of the Habsburg Empire.
- Nonetheless, the Organon was translated into Hungarian in 1830.
- A homeopathic hospital was opened in 1833 in Koszeg.
- The ban was lifted in 1837.
- In 1844, a department of homeopathy was established at the University of Pest.
- In 1865, the Hungarian Society of Homeopathic Physicians was founded.
- Around that time the first homeopathic journals appeared.
- In 1870, the first homeopathic hospital opened.
- Around the turn of the century, homeopathy went into a sharp decline.
- After the Second World War, homeopathy was once again banned in Hungary.
- In 1991, the Hungarian Society of Homeopathic Physicians was re-established.

From its early beginnings, homeopathy has attracted many unusual, charismatic personalities, and many of them had fascinating lives. Some of these personalities were discussed above, others like *Bier*, *Blackie*, *Boenninghausen*, *Boericke*, *Boiron*, *Bonneval*, *Jahr*, *Jennichen*, *Peschier*, *Stapf*, *Tessier*, *Ullman*, and *Vithoulkas* are mentioned in the second part of this book.

When studying their history, a striking fact emerges: almost all of the prominent homeopaths, including Hahnemann himself, were converted by a dramatic personal experience. Elsewhere I have called this curious phenomenon the homeopathic epiphany:

> Initiated by a highly emotional epiphany, their faith cannot be shaken by rational arguments […] True believers claim to have started out as sceptics and they often insist that they are driven by a scientific mind.

This seems to be true as much for the early followers of Hahnemann as it is for many of today's homeopaths.

Chapter 6
Different Types of Homeopathy and Homeopaths

In the previous chapter, we have seen that *Hahnemann* repeatedly insisted that his followers should adhere strictly to his teachings. Any deviation from his instructions was unacceptable to him, but these demands for absolute loyalty and unconditional obedience inevitably led to problems:

- Not all *homeopaths* became slavish followers of Hahnemann's dogma and some naturally developed their own ideas.
- Hahnemann's writings were full of contradictions which had the potential to confuse his followers; some homeopaths thus discarded some of Hahnemann's instructions, while adhering to others.
- In the light of many new and important scientific discoveries, much of what Hahnemann had once stated became obsolete; some homeopaths felt compelled to integrate this new knowledge into their practice.

It was thus almost unavoidable that, over the years, Hahnemann's original ideas got repeatedly modified. These developments soon led to the emergence of different schools of homeopathy. For instance, some homeopaths continued to believe in the *vital force* as postulated by Hahnemann, while others felt *vitalism* had no place in modern health care; some homeopaths thought that *ultra-high potencies* were the most *effective* remedies, while others doubted that they could be more than *placebos*.

In addition to these different 'schools of thought' within homeopathy, several true variations of homeopathy were developed. In consequence, homeopathy currently no longer consists of just a single, uniform therapeutic approach used by all homeopaths around the globe. Today, numerous forms of homeopathy exist side by side and each requires its own brief explanation.

© Springer International Publishing Switzerland 2016
E. Ernst, *Homeopathy - The Undiluted Facts*,
DOI 10.1007/978-3-319-43592-3_6

6.1   Variations of Homeopathy in Use Today

A range of different types of homeopathy are currently popular. The most important of these include:

- Auto-*isopathy*. This is treatment with remedies made from the patient's own body substances which have been *potentised* according to homeopathic manufacturing processes. An example is the use of pus from a patient for generating a homeopathic remedy to cure his disease.
- *Classical homeopathy*. The practice strictly based on Hahnemann's instructions (as described in the previous chapters), where each patient is treated according to his or her individual pattern of symptoms, clinical signs, and personal characteristics.
- *Clinical homeopathy*. This is non-individualised treatment based mainly on *guiding symptoms*, where the choice of the remedy depends not on the individual patient but on his diagnosis. A well-known example is the use of homeopathically prepared *arnica* for cuts and bruises, regardless of the individual characteristics of the patient.
- *Complex homeopathy*. Treatment with a combination of remedies containing a multitude of homeopathic remedies (Hahnemann insisted that only one remedy should be used for a given patient at any time); the combination is chosen such that the ingredients cover the most likely remedies of a given condition to the principals of clinical homeopathy.
- *Homotoxicology*. Treatment based on *Reckeweg's* concepts of *detoxification*.
- *Isopathy*. The use of remedies made by potentising the causative agent. An example is the use of a specific allergen (e.g., grass pollen) for the treatment of an allergy (e.g., hayfever). Strictly speaking, isopathy does not obey the *like cures like* principle, but it follows the assumption that 'identical cures identical'.

6.2   Popular Derivatives of Homeopathy

In addition to these relatively minor variations of the homeopathic theme, there are derivatives of it, i.e., therapeutic methods that were developed or strongly influenced by *homeopaths* to incorporate some of Hahnemann's concepts, but, at the same time, disregard several other of his basic principles. Consequently, most homeopaths would hesitate to call them homeopathy.

- *Anthroposophical* medicine is a health care system that was invented by Rudolf *Steiner* and Ita Wegman in the early 20th century. It is based on Steiner's metaphysical ideas about the different aspects of life, called anthroposophy. The preparations used are often diluted, like homeopathic remedies, but they are not potentised according to homeopathic rules.
- *Bach flower remedies* are remedies developed by Edward *Bach*, a medical doctor who worked for some time in the *Royal London Homeopathic Hospital*. When

he left this institution, he conceived a mystical notion of disease and, during the 1930s, developed a set of 38 flower remedies. These are highly diluted to the point where they no longer contain relevant amounts of the flowers they are based on, but they do not follow other homeopathic principles, such as the potentiation of remedies or the like cures like principle.

- *Schuessler salts* are low potency salts invented at the end of the 19th century by the German homeopath Wilhelm Heinrich *Schuessler* (1821–1898). They are based on 'tissue salts' and represent Schuessler's attempt to reconcile homeopathic concepts with Virchow's cellular pathology, which had just been discovered.

Further explanations are provided in part two of this book.

6.3 Different Attitudes of Practitioners

These different variations of homeopathy are employed, not just by homeopaths, but by people with entirely different professional backgrounds. Thus several different types of homeopaths can be differentiated. Below I try to characterise them and, based on an in-depth study of Hahnemann's writings, I will also attempt to speculate what Hahnemann might have felt about this practice.

The Purist Homeopath

Purist homeopaths follow Hahnemann's instructions religiously and employ homeopathy as the only therapeutic option for any symptom or disease they might treat. Hahnemann would, of course, have approved of such faithful disciples. Exact figures do not exist, but it seems that today the purist homeopath is in the minority.

The Liberal Homeopath

Despite explicit orders to the contrary, most homeopathic doctors today combine homeopathic remedies with all sorts of conventional medicines, and even many *lay* homeopaths consider this more liberal approach to be in the best interest of the patient. In the words of Hahnemann, these homeopaths are 'half-homeopaths' who have 'betrayed' his teachings. He would most certainly have disowned them; being convinced that the administration of other treatments weakens the power of his remedies, he would have predicted that their approach is doomed to failure.

The Occasional Homeopath

In several countries—Germany is a good example—doctors tend to use homeopathy only on relatively rare occasions. It seems that many of these clinicians do not really believe in the *effectiveness* of homeopathy; they might employ it merely because some patients ask for it, or because they want to use it as a legally and *ethically* defensible *placebo*.

There can be little doubt that Hahnemann would have condemned this approach. He would have regarded it as useless and would have called it 'treason' or worse.

The DIY Homeopath

Do-it-yourself homeopath is my term for describing patients and consumers who have no training in homeopathy whatsoever, but nevertheless buy homeopathic remedies over the counter and self-administer them without consulting a trained homeopath.

This group of individuals seems to be by far the largest of all types of homeopaths. Yet it is most certainly not one that Hahnemann would have condoned. Homeopathy is built on the *like cures like principle*. This means that the optimal remedy has to be identified by a skilled homeopath on the basis of a long and arduous study. Hahnemann would have called the DIY homeopaths fools and would most likely have tried to stop *pharmacists*—he had a life-long battle with this profession—selling his remedies to non-homeopaths.

A critical look at what is happening in homeopathy today and how it is being practised might arrive at somewhat confused conclusions. Hahnemann was quite clear about the importance of following his instructions to the letter. Very few homeopaths, however, seem to do that today. It follows that, given Hahnemann's stubbornness and intolerance of ideas that were not his own, he might disapprove or even disown the vast majority of today's homeopathy.

Chapter 7
The Patients of Homeopaths

Hahnemann advocated homeopathy for all human conditions or illnesses, and today many *homeopaths* still do exactly that; they recommend it for any illness or symptom that afflicts humans (or animals and even plants). However, this does not mean that patients who use homeopathy employ it whenever they fall ill. In fact, there is now a sizeable body of evidence about those who are likely to try homeopathy and for what conditions.

7.1 Who Is Likely to Try Homeopathy?

Much research has recently gone into answering this question. However, most of the key facts have been known for almost 40 years. An article of 1978 by Avina and Schneiderman summarised the issue clearly and correctly:

> [...] for the most part the patients are young, white and well-educated, and have white-collar jobs; most had previously tried mainstream medical care and found it unsatisfactory. Among the reasons for their dissatisfaction were instances of negative side effects from medication, lack of nutritional or preventive medical counselling, and lack of health education. Experiences with conventional physicians were almost evenly divided: nearly half of the subjects reported poor experiences, slightly fewer reported good experiences. Three quarters of the patients suffered from chronic illness and about half considered their progress to be good under homeopathic care. The majority were simultaneously involved in other non-traditional health care activities.

According to a flurry of survey data available today, the typical user of homeopathy is female, middle-aged, relatively affluent, and well-educated. That by no means implies that individuals who do not meet these criteria never try homeopathy; it merely describes the type of person who is most likely to give homeopathy a try.

Most homeopathic patients are on average younger and better educated than those opting to use conventional treatments. They tend to be involved in education, health

© Springer International Publishing Switzerland 2016
E. Ernst, *Homeopathy - The Undiluted Facts*,
DOI 10.1007/978-3-319-43592-3_7

care, and social services. Surprisingly, their factual knowledge of homeopathy is often minimal. Their general life attitudes tend to correspond to aspects of homeopathic philosophy. Homeopathic patients are more critical of medicine in general, and often have negative *experiences* with conventional medicine. They tend to choose homeopathy largely on the basis of their own experience and that of friends, family, and acquaintances. Most homeopathic patients enjoy good social support, recommend homeopathy to others, and regularly meet people who are also treated homeopathically. Dissatisfaction and negative experiences with conventional treatment may be one reason for turning to homeopathy initially. Reasons for continuing with this approach include its perceived *effectiveness*, good care by homeopaths, congruence with the patient's world view, and a feeling of responsibility for one's own health.

Typically, homeopathy users receive their information about homeopathy from friends, family, or the media. In most countries, the press has a remarkably keen interest in the subject, and there are millions of websites on the subject. Unfortunately, much of the information in the public domain is highly misleading and overtly promotional. On average, users of homeopathy adopt a healthier life-style than nonusers; they smoke less, consume less alcohol, eat a healthier diet, try to avoid stress, regularly get more sleep, and so on.

7.2   What Attracts Consumers to Homeopathy?

Many people are attracted to homeopathy because they see it as an effective and natural treatment that is virtually *risk*-free. They tend to like the notion that homeopaths practice a patient-centred, *holistic* approach and have more time for their patients than conventional clinicians. Patients treasure the quality of the *therapeutic relationship* with their homeopath as well as the *empathy* and *compassion* homeopaths are often able to offer.

Some users of homeopathy are frustrated with certain aspects of conventional medicine; in particular, they dislike the short *consultations* that conventional doctors normally offer, the fact that their treatments almost inevitably consist of writing a prescription for a pharmaceutical, the perceived de-humanisation of health care, and the all too often serious side-effects of conventional drugs. Comparing patients who consult *homeopaths* with those who prefer conventional doctors, Furnham and Smith found that:

> [...] the homeopathic group were much more critical and sceptical about the efficacy of traditional medicine; they believed that their general health could be improved; and they tended to have higher psychiatric morbidity.

7.3   What Diseases Do Users of Homeopathy Suffer From?

Homeopaths pride themselves on treating the patient and not his/her disease. *Classical homeopaths* who adhere to the teachings of Hahnemann might not even be interested in any conventional disease categories. Hahnemann believed that the nature of a disease is not knowable, and that the individual pattern of a patient's symptoms is the best guide to understanding and treating patients effectively. Therefore, classical homeopaths try to capture the totality of a patient's symptoms and find the remedy that optimally matches them. This explains why they would treat all or most patients in a way that pays no heed to the diseases they may suffer from.

A quote from a 2011 book entitled Homeopathy in Healthcare explains this in an exemplary fashion:

> Many acute and chronic conditions, especially in primary health care, can be treated homeo-pathically as long as the patient's regulatory and self-regulatory powers (*vital force*) can still be adequately stimulated. [...] Obvious limitations exist where there is a compelling indica-tion for substitution therapy (such as insulin for juvenile diabetes) or surgical intervention (with bone fractures, for instance), or with severe terminal pathologies were regulation is no longer possible. From the homeopathic point of view, surgical intervention is not always necessarily indicated and even with severe pathologies, *cost-effective* and side-effect free palliation and alleviation are possible.

Such views are mostly held by *lay homeopaths*. *Medical homeopaths* who may be following Hahnemann's dictum less slavishly will accept conventional diagnoses and treat their patients accordingly, with either conventional or homeopathic means. However, there are few conditions for which they would not employ homeopathy, if only as a complementary therapy.

Common diseases which bring patients to a homeopath include depression, anx-iety, pain, allergies, asthma, common cold, *flu*, diarrhoea, hay fever, constipation, cough, otitis, measles, mumps, chickenpox, whooping cough, eczema, shingles, psoriasis, piles, and many others. In a 2001, survey of *professional organisations* of homeopathy, we asked about the conditions that responded best to homeopathic treatments; the replies indicated that respiratory, menstrual, rheumatic, and skin prob-lems were deemed to be at the top of the list.

The Australian Homeopathic Association answered the question 'What conditions can homeopathy treat?' as follows:

> Homeopathy aims to treat the whole person, taking into account personality, lifestyle and hereditary factors as well as the history of the disease. Since all patients are unique, home-opathic medicines are prescribed to treat patients as individuals. For example, headaches in different patients would each be treated with different medicines, according to the patient's individual symptoms. Homeopathy can be of benefit at any stage of life: men, women, moth-ers, fathers, very young and older children, teenagers, and the elderly. It may be used in the management of a wide range of conditions including, for example:
>
> - Acute complaints: coughs, colds, ear-ache, food poisoning, hangover, travel sickness, etc.
> - Chronic complaints: skin conditions, hormone imbalances, mood swings, headaches, behavioural problems, digestive disturbances, arthritis, etc.
> - First aid situations: bites, stings, hives, injuries, trauma, emotional shock, etc.
> - Vague symptoms: where there are no identifiable causes of disease, but the person feels far from well.
>
> The system of homeopathy is based on the selection of a medicine that causes symptoms similar to those that the sick person is experiencing. This *Law of Similars*, as it is called, is a practical method of finding the substance to which a person is sensitive. Wherever

a set of symptoms can be obtained, a condition can be treated. For example, headaches in different patients would each be managed with different medicines, according to the patient's individual symptoms.

To many responsible health care professionals, such statements are deeply worrying; they give the impression that even serious health problems can be effectively treated with homeopathy. As we will see in Chap. 9, the *evidence* that this might be true is less than convincing.

Chapter 8
Homeopathy as a Criticism of Conventional Medicine

The current popularity of homeopathy amazes many health care professionals and annoys experts who are sceptical about the virtues of *alternative medicine*. Why do people use treatments which are both implausible and not *evidence*-based, they ask? Why do they opt for something that is questionable and arguably obsolete at a time when health care has become better than it has ever been? As we have seen in previous chapters, there are several answers to these questions. One important reason for today's popularity of homeopathy is clearly that many patients are not impressed with what modern medicine has to offer.

Some time ago, we published a *systematic review* of *surveys* aimed at identifying what patients hope for when they consult practitioners of alternative medicine. In order of importance, the most common issues that emerged from this research were patients' hope for:

- fewer side-effects,
- symptom relief,
- cure of their disease,
- ability to cope better with their condition,
- improvements in quality of life,
- a boost to the immune system,
- prevention of illness,
- good therapeutic relationship with a clinician,
- holistic care,
- emotional support,
- control over their own health.

This begs the question: to what extent are patients driven to see *homeopaths* simply because conventional medicine is letting them down? Several of the expectations named in the list above are implicit criticisms of conventional medicine and the way it tends to be practised today. This gets even clearer if the above points are slightly rephrased. According to our findings, patients seem to feel:

© Springer International Publishing Switzerland 2016
E. Ernst, *Homeopathy - The Undiluted Facts*,
DOI 10.1007/978-3-319-43592-3_8

- that conventional treatments have too many side-effects,
- that they frequently fail to ease their symptoms,
- that they often do not cure the disease,
- that conventional doctors do not enable their patients to cope with their condition,
- that conventional doctors do not care enough about their patients' *quality of life*,
- that many conventional approaches neglect the importance of stimulating the immune system to fend off disease,
- that *prevention* is not given the importance it should have in medicine,
- that conventional doctors often fail to establish good *therapeutic relationships* with their patients,
- that conventional doctors tend to ignore the fact that their patients are not just 'cases' but whole human *individuals*,
- that conventional doctors are often not providing enough emotional support,
- that they fail to empower their patients with control of their own health.

All too often, the failings of modern medicine seem as obvious as they seem inexcusable. It is thus understandable that some disappointed patients seek help and *compassion* from homeopaths. Seen from this perspective, the current popularity of homeopathy indicates that many patients are not satisfied with what conventional medicine offers. In other words, the current boom in homeopathy can be seen as a poignant criticism of certain aspects of modern health care.

8.1 The Therapeutic Relationship

Many people find modern medicine too technical, impersonal, and often even heartless; similarly, they feel that too many conventional doctors are lacking in *compassion* and *empathy*. To a very large extent this is a question of the time available for building up a therapeutic relationship. A normal *consultation* with a general practitioner usually lasts less than ten minutes. This lack of time deeply frustrates patients, as it rarely offers enough opportunity for a warm and constructive therapeutic relationship to develop. What is more, during such short consultations, many physicians seem to pay more attention to their computer than to the individual in front of them. At the end, many patients feel palmed off with a prescription before they were able to express all of their problems, concerns, and worries. They get the impression that their wish to be in charge of their own health is largely ignored.

The situation is dramatically different when they see their homeopath. Here, a consultation can last one hour or more, there is plenty of time to talk about whatever issue might be important to the patient. The homeopath listens patiently, shows *compassion* and empathy, asks questions which conventional clinicians would never think of, offers seemingly plausible explanations for the symptoms, and discusses any therapeutic approach in full detail with his patient. As a result, patients feel empowered as partners in their own health and holistically cared for as unique individuals, mind, body, and soul.

It is thus not in the least surprising that patients rate the quality of the therapeutic relationship with their homeopath significantly higher than that with their conventional doctor. Patients usually treasure the human aspects of homeopathy very highly. For many of them, the homeopathic remedy is of secondary importance, while the time, understanding, and emotional support that homeopaths manage to offer is what they need in order to cope with their illness.

8.2 Ineffective Drugs

In the past, many hugely exaggerated promises have been made about the future of modern medicine. For many consumers they seemed to raise the hope that we might soon be approaching an age of universal good health. However, the reality turned out to be very different. The suffering of too many patients continued more or less unabated. Their *quality of life* remained impaired, their hope for a cure got harshly disappointed, and their treatments were burdened with significant side-effects which often seemed to make matters even worse. In some cases, modern medicine turned apparently healthy individuals into patients with symptoms. For instance, a perfectly symptom-free patient might consult his/her doctor, who would subsequently diagnose hypercholesterolemia and prescribe statins; as a result of taking this medication, the patient might suffer from all sorts of symptoms and even develop muscle pain or liver problems.

Today, many patients are bitterly disappointed with what they perceive as the broken promises of modern medicine. Marked by this *experience*, they look for other solutions to their problems and often find them in the form of homeopathy. If they hear about the considerable doubts regarding the *effectiveness* of homeopathic remedies, they merely shrug their shoulders. Modern medicine has helped them little; homeopathy, they feel, offers at least the compassion and sympathy they crave. Even if the remedies have little or no effect, compassion alone may suffice to ease their suffering and improving their well-being.

8.3 Risks of Modern Medicine

Yet conventional medicine has made huge progress since the days of *Hahnemann*. Uncounted therapies have been developed and many of them can cure or at least alleviate previously difficult to treat conditions. But, of course, none of these treatments is without side-effects. Hospitals are filled with people who require help because of the adverse effects of medical interventions. It is estimated that globally 142 000 people died in 2013 from the effects of medical treatments. The risks of modern medicine include:

- side-effects of drugs,
- drug/drug interactions,

- complications arising from procedures,
- medical errors,
- negligence by health care professionals.

In his 1974 book Medical Nemesis: The Expropriation of Health, Ivan Illich broadened the scope of harm even further by defining three different risk-categories of modern healthcare:

- Clinical iatrogenesis is the injury done to patients by ineffective, unsafe, and erroneous treatments.
- Social iatrogenesis describes the medicalization of life in which the medical industry creates unrealistic health demands that require more and more treatments for conditions that do not necessarily require any treatment at all; the results are over-diagnosis and over-treatment.
- Cultural iatrogenesis, finally, refers to the destruction of traditional values and ways of dealing with or making sense of illness, suffering, sickness, and death.

Many consumers have become keenly aware of these issues and want to opt out of the 'medical nemesis'. One way of doing this is to consult a *homeopath*. Most consumers seem to feel that homeopathic remedies are gentle and largely free of risks, that homeopaths do not belong to the medical industry, and that they uphold traditional ways of healing.

The expectations, fears, and assumptions of consumers may frequently be misguided or wrong, yet it is hard to deny that they can be deeply felt, and it seems obvious that, in such cases, they can contribute significantly to the popularity of homeopathy.

Chapter 9
Scientific Evidence

9.1 What Is Evidence and What Is Not?

Many homeopaths feel that the daily *experience* of thousands of *homeopaths* (and millions of patients) holds information about the *effectiveness* of homeopathy which is more reliable than any scientific investigation. When their patients get better, they assume this to be the result of their treatment. Eventually, they become convinced that their experience is more trustworthy than *evidence*.

Yet such a conclusion might be erroneous. The reason is simple: two events—the treatment by the homeopath and the improvement of the patient—that follow each other in time are not necessarily causally related. The *natural history of the condition*, *regression towards the mean*, the *placebo effect* are just a few of the phenomena that can determine the clinical outcome in such a way that inefficacious or even mildly harmful treatments appear to be effective. *Hufeland*, the famous contemporary of *Hahnemann*, summed it up well:

> After 30 years of practice, I am fully convinced that two thirds of all my patients would have recovered without the use of physic, or the attendance of a physician.

What follows from such considerations could not be clearer: the prescribed treatment is only one of several factors that influence the clinical *outcome*, and a positive clinical experience with homeopathy—or any other treatment—can be misleading.

Homeopaths are often incredulous when someone tries to explain to them how little their experience tells us about the effectiveness of their remedies and usually come up with several counter-arguments:

- The improvement was so prompt that it was evidently caused by my treatment [this notion is not convincing; placebo effects can be just as prompt].
- I have seen it so many times that it cannot be a coincidence [homeopaths tend to be very caring, charismatic, and *empathetic* and would thus regularly generate powerful placebo responses].

© Springer International Publishing Switzerland 2016
E. Ernst, *Homeopathy - The Undiluted Facts*,
DOI 10.1007/978-3-319-43592-3_9

- A study with several thousand patients shows that over 70 % of them improved with homeopathy [such response rates are typical, even for ineffective treatments, particularly in situations where patient *expectation* is high].
- Chronic conditions don't suddenly get better without an effective treatment; the natural history of the disease is therefore not a plausible explanation for the observed improvement [this is incorrect; eventually, many chronic conditions improve, if only temporarily].
- I had a patient with a serious condition, I prescribed homeopathy and she was cured [if one investigates such cases, one often finds that the patient also took conventional treatments; moreover, in rare instances, even patients with serious conditions such as cancer experience spontaneous remissions].
- I have tried homeopathy myself and had a positive result [clinicians are not immune to placebo or other non-specific effects].
- Even children and *animals* respond to homeopathy. Surely they are not prone to placebo effects [animals and children can be conditioned to respond; and then there are, of course, phenomena such as the natural history of the disease as well as the placebo effect by proxy].

The fact that personal experience is not the same as scientific evidence does not mean that it is useless. It is invaluable for a lot of other things, but it never constitutes proof of therapeutic effectiveness.

Because the outcomes after medical treatments always have many determinants, we need a different approach for testing treatments. The multifactorial nature of any clinical response necessitates controlling for all the factors that might determine the outcome other than the treatment per se. Ideally, we need an experiment where two groups of patients are exposed to the full range of these factors, and the only difference between them is that one group does receive the treatment, while the other does not.

This is precisely the concept of a controlled *clinical trial*. This simple research tool accounts for all or most of the factors which might otherwise cloud our judgement. In a typical controlled clinical trial of homeopathy, researchers divide a group of patients (or healthy volunteers or animals) into one subgroup who are given homeopathic remedies and a second subgroup, called the control group, which receives a different treatment, for instance, a placebo or a conventional therapy (the choice depends on the precise research question). Subsequently, the two treatments are administered for the prescribed length of time. At the end of this period, the results of the two groups are compared. If the homeopathic group demonstrates superior outcomes to the placebo group, the homeopathic remedy was effective, otherwise it was *ineffective*, i.e., not better than placebo.

Many different variations of the controlled trial exist, and the exact design can be adapted to the requirements of the specific research question at hand. The overriding aim, however, should always be the same: to make sure that we can reliably determine whether or not the treatment was the cause of the observed outcome.

Causality is, of course, the key in all of this; and it is the crucial difference between clinical experience and scientific evidence. The outcomes clinicians witness in their practice can have a myriad of causes. By contrast, what scientists observe in a well-designed trial is, in all likelihood, caused by the treatment. The latter is evidence, while the former is not.

Yet clinical trials are not perfect. They can have flaws and have rightly been criticised for a myriad of inherent limitations. But, despite all their shortcomings, they are far superior to any other currently known method for determining the effectiveness of medical interventions.

Since clinical trials can occasionally produce false results, we should avoid relying on the findings of a single study. Independent replications are usually required to be sure. Unfortunately, the findings of such replications do not always confirm the results of the previous study, and therefore we often have a confusing array of findings. This is precisely the situation we find in homeopathy.

Whenever we are faced with conflicting results, it is tempting to *cherry-pick* those studies which seem to confirm our prior belief—tempting but wrong. In order to arrive at the most reliable conclusion, we need to consider the totality of the reliable evidence. This goal is best achieved by conducting a *systematic review*.

In a systematic review, we assess the quality and quantity of the available evidence, try to synthesise the findings, and arrive at an overall verdict. Technically speaking, this process minimises selection and random *biases*. Systematic reviews (and *meta-analyses*, i.e., systematic reviews that pool the data of individual studies and calculate a new quantitative result) therefore constitute the best available evidence for or against the effectiveness of homeopathy or any other treatment.

Why is evidence important? In a way, this question has already been answered: only with reliable evidence can we tell with any degree of certainty that it was the homeopathic remedy per se—and not one of the other factors mentioned above—that caused the clinical outcome we observe in a patient or group of patients. Only if we have such evidence can we be sure about cause and effect. And only then can we make sure that patients receive the best treatments currently available.

There are, of course, those who say that causality does not matter all that much. What is important, they claim, is to help the patient, and if it was a placebo-effect that did the trick, who cares? This attitude is misguided for several reasons. To mention just one, we would probably all agree that the placebo effect can benefit many patients, yet it would be a *fallacy* to assume that we need a placebo treatment to generate a placebo response. If a clinician administers an effective therapy (one that generates benefit beyond placebo) with *compassion*, time, empathy, and understanding, she will generate a placebo response plus a response to the therapy administered. It follows that, merely administering a placebo is less than optimal; in fact, it usually means preventing the patient from benefitting from an effective therapy.

9.2 The Scientific Evidence for or Against Homeopathy

Mechanism of Action

For 200 years now, critics of homeopathy have been keen to point out that Hahnemann's assumptions are not biologically plausible. The *like cures like principle*, they insist, may apply to certain circumstances, but it is not a general *law* of nature. Even more criticism is aimed at the idea that water has a *memory* and that *diluting* a substance might thus render it more potent.

According to *Avogadro*, all homeopathic remedies beyond the C12 *potency* are too dilute to contain even a single molecule of the *mother tincture*. Yet homeopaths believe that they are potent medicines. Some homeopaths admit that they cannot explain why this is so and that the *mechanism of action* of homeopathic remedies is not known. Hahnemann himself postulated that their "action must be called spirit-like". This assumption is based on the concept of *vitalism*, a philosophy which is today obsolete. Hahnemann believed that disease is a derangement of the body's vital force; modern science shows us that this is a metaphysical concept that is simply not true.

Today many homeopaths have moved on and point to *basic science* studies which, in their opinion, might go some way towards providing a rational explanation for homeopathy's mechanism of action. For instance, some experiments have suggested that water molecules can, in fact, form structures which might preserve the memory of the substances previously contained in that water. Other homeopaths believe that, during the process of succussion, tiny particles, called *nanoparticles*, are formed, which in turn explain the health effects of highly diluted remedies. Others again think that *hormesis*—the phenomenon that, at very low doses, some toxins can have the opposite effects from those at high doses—could provide a scientific explanation for homeopathy's mechanism of action. Unfortunately, all of these theories have one very obvious thing in common: they are just *theories*! As such they are shared by some but not by the majority of scientists, and a scientific consensus as to how homeopathy works simply does not exist at the moment. In fact, if we are close to a consensus, it would be that there is no explanation for homeopathy's mechanism of action (other than a placebo effect) which would be in keeping with the known laws of nature.

Those experts who doubt that homeopathic remedies have any effects beyond those of placebo are convinced that the benefit patients experience after seeing a homeopath are due to non-specific effects, e.g., the empathetic consultation with a homeopath, placebo effects, regression towards the mean, or the natural history of the disease (see below).

Effectiveness

Many homeopaths argue that it may be desirable to understand how a treatment works but, for clinical routine, this is actually not necessary. Aspirin helped millions of patients long before we knew its mechanism of action, for instance. This argument is undoubtedly true. It is conceivable that we simply do not comprehend the way homeopathic remedies bring about their effects, and this is why the question 'How does it work?' is less important than 'Does it work?'

Homeopaths tend to feel that the 200-year history of homeopathy and its current popularity have already resolved the issue. They suggest that their patients would simply not come back if their remedies were not effective, and they stress that their collective experience, in addition to dozens of *observational studies*, are sufficient proof. But such arguments fail to satisfy the more sceptical experts who insist on solid evidence.

In the early days of homeopathy, the emerging evidence for homeopathy seemed encouraging. In particular, in the treatment of large *epidemics*, homeopathy appeared to generate significantly better outcomes than conventional treatments. While such findings naturally enthused homeopaths, they failed to impress critics who pointed out that a range of reasons unrelated to any effect of the homeopathic remedies might explain the results.

The most reliable method to find out whether a treatment is effective or not is to conduct a controlled clinical trial. The very first randomised, placebo-controlled, double-blind test of homeopathy—one of the very first such studies in the history of medicine—was carried out in 1835 by the Gesellschaft Wahrheitsliebender Maenner (Society of truth-loving men) of Nuremberg. Its results showed no difference in response between a homeopathic remedy and the placebo.

Today about 300 such trials have been published. Unsurprisingly, their findings are not entirely uniform; some studies show a positive result but many do not. Faced with such contradictions, it might be tempting to *cherry-pick*. A recent report, often alleged to be by the Swiss government, is frequently cited by homeopaths as being equivalent or even superior to a *systematic review*. It concluded that, for certain conditions, homeopathic treatment is effective. However, a critical assessment of this report finds reasons to doubt its conclusions. It is not by the Swiss government; in fact, it was written by 13 advocates of homeopathy who have no connection with any government. They decided to employ their own, unusual criteria for what constitutes evidence. For instance, they included *case reports* and *case series*, redefined what is meant by effectiveness, cherry-picked the articles they included, and assessed only a very narrow range of indications. This report cannot therefore be taken as reliable evidence.

Systematic reviews avoid cherry-picking and include a *critical analysis* of the included data. Today, about 50 systematic reviews of homeopathy have been published. In order to avoid cherry-picking on this level, it is therefore necessary to summarise the totality of all such articles. Exactly this has recently been done by a panel of independent experts, the National Health and Medicine Research Council (*NHMRC*) of Australia. They stated that:

> [...] based on the assessment of the evidence of effectiveness of homeopathy, NHMRC concludes that there are no health conditions for which there is reliable evidence that homeopathy is effective.

Economic Analyses of Homeopathy

Homeopathic remedies are generally far cheaper than conventional drugs and this prompts some homeopaths to claim that money could be saved if we used more homeopathy. This argument might look convincing at first sight, but when scrutinised, it turns out to be naïve and misleading.

Researchers from the University of Sheffield recently published a systematic review of all *economic evaluations* of homeopathy. They included 14 such studies in their review and concluded that:

> [...] although the identified evidence of the costs and potential benefits of homeopathy seemed promising, studies were highly heterogeneous and had several methodological weaknesses. It is therefore not possible to draw firm conclusions based on existing economic evaluations of homeopathy.

These investigators also pointed out that most of the studies were of poor methodological quality and therefore their findings were not reliable. More recently, a cost-effectiveness analysis has been published which is by far the most rigorous to date. Ostermann and coworkers analysed cost data from 44 550 patients who had either opted to use homeopathy or to employ just conventional medicine. The results show that the total costs after 18 months were higher in the homeopathy group than in the control group. The largest differences between groups were in the areas of productivity loss and outpatient care costs. For all diagnoses, costs were higher for patients who had chosen homeopathy compared to those who had used conventional health care. The investigators concluded that:

> [...] compared with usual care, additional homeopathic treatment was associated with significantly higher costs.

Risk/Benefit Analysis

Any therapy has to be judged, not just on its effectiveness, but also on its *risks*. If the former does not outweigh the latter, the *risk/benefit analysis* cannot be positive, and consequently the treatment in question would probably not be recommended for routine use.

Homeopathy has an image of being entirely risk-free. However, this assumption may not be entirely correct. In fact, there are several areas of concern:

- *Low potency* remedies can contain large amounts of the material of the *mother tincture*. If the mother tincture happens to be toxic, low potency remedies will be toxic as well. In this context, one expert has concluded that:

  > [...] homeopathic products containing active agents in allopathic doses should be treated the same way as *allopathic* medicines from the point of view of quality assurance and pharmacovigilance.

  In most countries, this is sadly not the case, and consumers can be put at considerable risk by such preparations.
- After administering their treatment, homeopaths frequently expect an acute worsening of a patient's symptoms, a phenomenon they call homeopathic *aggravation*.
- As the quality control procedures of some countries are less than rigorous, some homeopathic remedies may be contaminated with substances that might be toxic.
- Hahnemann insisted that homeopathy must not be combined with conventional treatments. Even today, some homeopaths insist that homeopathy is an appropriate

alternative for serious conditions including cancer. For instance, one of the most influential *lay homeopaths* today, George *Vithoulkas*, wrote in 1998:

> No allopathic drugs should be taken at the same time as the homeopathic treatment.

If such statements prevent consumers or patients from using effective interventions in a timely fashion, serious harm can ensue. The above-mentioned NHMRC report therefore concluded that:

> [...] people who choose homeopathy may put their health at risk if they reject or delay treatments for which there is good evidence for safety and effectiveness.

It follows, that, contrary to what is often claimed, the use of homeopathy is not entirely free of risk. The risks may be small—they are certainly smaller than the risks of many conventional treatments—but they undeniably exist. If we then consider that, according to the most thorough analysis, homeopathy's effectiveness is in doubt, a risk/benefit analysis of homeopathy is unlikely to generate a positive conclusion. In other words, homeopathy has not been shown to generate more good than harm.

Chapter 10
Spurious Arguments for and Counter-Arguments Against Homeopathy

The disputes between those who love and those who loathe homeopathy have lasted for as long as homeopathy exists. In the past, they have often generated more heat than light, and today the two camps often seem to be as far apart as ever. To some extent, this lack of progress is due to the fact that many arguments seem logical at first sight but turn out to be *fallacious* on closer inspection.

This chapter picks up the theme from Chap. 3, where the myths in and around homeopathy were listed. Now, with the insights gained from all the previous chapters, I intend to revisit some of them and review the most common spurious arguments from both sides of the divide. Crucially, I will try to contrast them with the current knowledge and scientific facts. In this way, I aim to summarise much of the content of this book and to contribute to rendering future debates about homeopathy more rational and better informed. My hope is that, after 200 years of largely futile discussions, progress might finally be made.

10.1 Spurious Arguments by Proponents of Homeopathy

1. Clinical Trials of Homeopathy Are Not Possible

Some *homeopaths* claim that their treatment is not amenable to being tested in rigorously controlled trials. They give several reasons for this notion, including:

- homeopathy is a highly *individualised* therapy,
- homeopaths do not treat diagnoses but individuals,
- homeopathy addresses the whole person,
- homeopathy follows a different *paradigm*.

Perhaps the best way to counter this argument is to point out that dozens of *clinical trials* of homeopathy have been published which do accommodate all or most of these

© Springer International Publishing Switzerland 2016
E. Ernst, *Homeopathy - The Undiluted Facts*,
DOI 10.1007/978-3-319-43592-3_10

concerns and features. Thus the argument turns out to be based on an insufficient understanding of what is achievable with the methodology of a clinical trial and its many variations.

2. More Placebo-Controlled Clinical Trials of Homeopathy Are Positive than Negative

Realising the importance of clinical trials, several pro-homeopathic organisations and individuals have claimed that the majority of the numerous *placebo*-controlled clinical trials of homeopathy available to date have generated positive results. This, they claim, indicates or even proves that homeopathy is indeed *effective*.

The argument turns out to be based on a simple accounting trick: statistics supporting it divide the trials into three categories: (1) positive, (2) negative, and (3) inconclusive. The first category comprises all the studies suggesting homeopathy to be superior to placebo; the second includes all the trials where placebo turned out to be superior to homeopathy; and the third (and by far the largest) category is composed of those studies which showed no difference between homeopathy and placebo. As few trials demonstrate that a placebo is better than homeopathy, the figures do indeed demonstrate that category 1 is larger than category 2.

However, this result is achieved through a rather inventive and unusual categorisation of the studies: placebo-controlled trials test whether a given treatment is better than a placebo. The answer can only be 'yes' or 'no'—the trials in category 3 are therefore not inconclusive, they are negative: they do not show homeopathy to be better than placebo. Once we do the proper accounting of these figures by merging categories 2 and 3 into one category of negative trials, we find that the majority of trials of homeopathy are in fact negative.

3. Homeopathy Works on Small Children

The argument here is that babies cannot have *expectations* regarding medical interventions and therefore cannot display a placebo response. As they do nevertheless respond to homeopathy, the effect must be proof that homeopathic remedies are not just placebos.

There are two separate errors here. Firstly, studies on babies can show a placebo response. For instance, the outcome of a treatment might be reported not by the infant but by a parent who undoubtedly can be susceptible to expectations. Secondly, it is by no means proven that homeopathy is effective in children. The only *systematic review* of this subject concluded, on the basis of all 16 studies available at the time, that:

> [...] the evidence from rigorous clinical trials of any type of therapeutic or preventive intervention testing homeopathy for childhood and adolescence ailments is not convincing enough for recommendations in any condition.

4. Homeopathy Works on Animals

Similar arguments and counter-arguments apply to the effects of homeopathy on *animals*. Firstly, it is not true that animals do not respond to placebos; in fact, part of the phenomenon that constitutes the placebo response, classical *conditioning*, was discovered by Pavlov in dogs. Secondly, it is wrong to assume that the effectiveness of homeopathy in animals is proven. The most up-to-date systematic review on this subject concluded that there is:

> [...] very limited evidence that clinical intervention in animals using homeopathic medicines is distinguishable from corresponding intervention using placebos.

5. Homeopathy Has Proven its Effectiveness in Major Epidemics

It is true that several reports exist suggesting that the use of homeopathy generated remarkably good results when employed in *epidemics*. However, if we have a closer look at such findings, we invariably discover many reasons, other than the alleged effectiveness of the homeopathic remedies, to account for the observed outcomes.

In the early days of homeopathy, the harmful *heroic* treatments of mainstream medicine meant that those patients who managed to escape conventional physicians by becoming the patients of homeopaths had better chances of survival. Later epidemiological reports have similar weaknesses; the groups of patients treated homeopathically are usually not comparable to those receiving conventional therapies, and the differences between them invariably suffice to explain why the former had better outcomes than the latter. In order to make a convincing case for homeopathy's effectiveness, we do not need epidemiological data, but we require *evidence* from controlled clinical studies—and this, as we have seen elsewhere in this book, fails to show that homeopathy is effective.

6. Homeopathy Has Never Been Proven Wrong

Some people point out that there is no conclusive *scientific* proof that homeopathy does not work. The seemingly clever slogan that is often used is: absence of evidence is no proof for evidence of absence. Until such poof exists, they claim, homeopathy should be used by and recommended to patients.

Superficially, this argument sounds logical. At closer inspection, we find, however, that it neglects two important issues: firstly, science is rarely an adequate tool to prove a negative. It is therefore virtually impossible to provide a scientific proof that homeopathy does not work. Secondly, we must remember that, in health care, we should always try to employ those methods for which positive proof exists, while avoiding those for which it is missing.

7. There Is a Worldwide Conspiracy against Homeopathy

Some advocates of homeopathy misunderstand criticism of their favourite therapy as a *conspiracy* organised by powerful, dark forces. The culprit behind such alleged intrigues is often assumed to be the pharmaceutical industry. 'Big Pharma' is, according to this assumption, so impressed by the effectiveness of homeopathic medicines that it has to take action against them or else their profits would dwindle and their shareholders would protest.

I have never seen any evidence for such alleged conspiracies; on the contrary, I do know of significant sections of the pharmaceutical industry that try to profit from the boom in homeopathic sales. Whenever I ask a conspiracy theorist to show me any evidence for his claims, I do not receive any. Until we see reliable evidence for conspiracies against homeopathy, we should conclude that the assumption of a conspiracy is more likely based on paranoia than on fact.

8. The Allegation that Homeopathy Is Implausible Is Incorrect

Many homeopaths cite elaborate *theories* to support their notion that the principles of homeopathy, particularly the *potentisation* of homeopathic remedies, is not nearly as implausible as *critics* would claim. They cite 'cutting edge' findings from *basic research* into pharmacology, or the structure of water molecules, or *nanoparticles*, or quantum physics to demonstrate that potentised solutions do behave differently than non-potentised solutions. Such arguments seem to forget a range of important issues:

- Any explanation of the *memory of water* becomes irrelevant when homeopathic remedies are issued not in liquid form but as water-free globuli.
- Even if potentised solutions differed from non-potentised solutions, one would still need to explain how exactly this difference might lead to significant effects on human health.
- None of the current assumptions to explain the activity of homeopathic remedies has gone beyond the stage of a theory, and none has been accepted by a consensus of expert opinion outside the realm of homeopathy.
- The various theories about a *mechanism of action* compete with each other; if one explained how homeopathy works, the others would necessarily be false. At present, not even homeopaths seem to be able to tell us which of the many theories might be correct and which are wrong.

9. Homeopathy Works like Vaccination

This is a popular argument in debates about the alleged mechanism of action of homeopathic remedies. It holds that *vaccines* are as highly *diluted* as homeopathic preparations, and points out that there is no doubt about the effectiveness of vaccinations; therefore, it is unreasonable to question homeopathic remedies on the grounds that they are highly diluted.

Even though the argument seems logical, it is nevertheless erroneous. Firstly, vaccines do unquestionably contain measurable amounts of active ingredients, while most homeopathic remedies do not. Secondly, vaccines work by generating measurable immune responses in the recipient, while no such responses have been observed after taking homeopathic remedies.

10. Many Conventional Medicines Are also Not Evidence-Based

This is, of course, true. Advocates of homeopathy claim that it is therefore not fair to demand a solid evidence base for homeopathic remedies. This merely reveals, they feel, double standards and *bias* against their favourite therapy.

Again, the notion seems convincing, particularly to lay people, but it is nevertheless fallacious: the fact that things are not optimal in one area, cannot be a justification for deficits in another field. In a nutshell, the argument is akin to promoting flying carpets because of the imperfections of the airline industry.

11. Just Because We Don't Know How Homeopathy Works Does Not Mean that It Is Ineffective

Some people point out that we often do not understand how a treatment works, but we nevertheless use it simply because it helps patients. The example that is commonly given is aspirin: for many years, we did not know the mode of action of this drug, but we still used it because it evidently did work. The argument is intriguing but also misleading: we would, of course, use homeopathy, if we had good evidence (as we had for aspirin, even when we failed to comprehend its mechanism of action) that it was more effective than placebo. However, this evidence is currently missing. Moreover, it is misleading to say we don't understand how homeopathic remedies work; the truth is that we do know that there cannot be an explanation as to how highly diluted homeopathic remedies work which does not contradict our understanding of nature.

12. Even Noble Prize Winners Support Homeopathy

It amounts to nothing less than a logical *fallacy* to claim that, because famous, prominent, or intelligent people do something, it must be good. Famous, prominent, and intelligent people are also prone to making mistakes, particularly when they find themselves outside their area of expertise. Moreover, many Nobel Prize winners and other VIPs have also been scathing about homeopathy.

13. Homeopathy Users Are Not Stupid

This is the indignant defence employed by users of homeopathy who claim that they do not need 'clever' scientists to tell them what type of treatment works for them; they know this well enough. The argument neglects the fact that, as pointed out elsewhere in this book, many phenomena can make an ineffective treatment appear to be effective: the *placebo effect*, *regression towards the mean*, and the *natural history* of the disease, to mention just three.

14. Homeopathy Is Sold in Major and Reputable Pharmacies So It Must Be Good

This is yet another fallacy. Not every product sold via reputable sources is credible, and not every credible product comes from a reputable source.

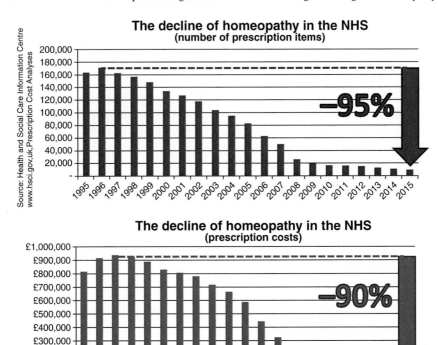

Fig. 10.1 Decline in the prescription of homeopathy in the NHS, UK. With permission of the Nightingale Collaboration

15. Homeopathy Is Reimbursed by Some National Health Systems

This is evidently true but the decision to cover the *expenditure* for medical interventions is determined by a host of factors, for instance, consumer demand (see Fig. 10.1). It can never serve as a substitute for evidence.

16. Thousands of Physicians Use Homeopathy

The 'ad populum' fallacy comes in many guises and can easily mislead us. The truth, however, is that the history of medicine is full of therapies which were once used by most physicians and many patients. Eventually, when they were critically evaluated and scientifically tested, they turned out to be useless or even harmful. Subsequently, they became obsolete, and many lives were saved through this development.

17. Homeopathy Has Stood the Test of Time

The same applies to the 'ad traditionem' fallacy. Bloodletting is just one of many examples of a treatment that was used for hundreds of years, and it was only when *scientific* scrutiny was applied to it that it became clear that it was useless and often even harmful. It had stood the test of time, but this test is unfortunately next to useless.

18. At Least Homeopathic Remedies Are Safe

This statement may be true but it is also not very relevant. The value of a treatment is not just determined by its *risks* but also by its *effectiveness*. There are many treatments which are burdened with horrendous side-effects, and yet, if they save lives, few people would hesitate to use them. It is the *risk/benefit* balance of a medical intervention that best informs our therapeutic decisions, and it cannot be positive, if the treatment in question is not effective—even if it is entirely *safe*.

19. Even If It Were a Placebo, Homeopathy Still Helps Many Patients

Some proponents of homeopathy point out that many people experience benefit from homeopathy. Even if this benefit were due to nothing else but a placebo effect, it would still be positive, because placebo effects also help patients. This argument is intuitively convincing and therefore difficult to oppose, even though several rational counter-arguments do exist and reveal it to be fallacious.

One might, for instance, point out that health care professionals must always be honest and *ethical*. If homeopaths follow this rule, they must inform their patients that their remedies are, in fact, placebos. This information would probably prevent the patient from experiencing a placebo effect, or even from trying the remedy in the first place.

A more convincing counter-argument might be to explain that administering an effective treatment with *compassion* will generate, not just a placebo effect, but also the therapeutic effect of the therapy. In other words, we do not necessarily need a placebo to generate a placebo effect, and relying solely on a placebo does not provide the optimal benefit for the patient.

20. Only Homeopaths Understand Homeopathy Well Enough

Whenever someone criticises homeopathy, *homeopaths* claim that the critic does not understand enough about the subject; as his criticism is not well-informed, it cannot be valid. This means that only expert homeopaths are able to voice a competent critique of homeopathy. An expert homeopath is, of course, someone who does not fundamentally object to homeopathy. This means we are confronted with the perfect circular argument; it essentially holds that valid criticism can never exist.

10.2   Spurious Arguments by Opponents of Homeopathy

The spurious arguments used by some opponents of homeopathy are less numerous than those employed by its proponents. Yet they are important because they can mislead the public and, of course, alienate homeopaths and their supporters, thus preventing a better understanding of the two camps and a more constructive debate.

1. In Its 200-Year History, Homeopathy Has Done No Good at all

As already pointed out in previous chapters, *Hahnemann* and his followers can be credited with considerable achievements. First and foremost, 200 years ago they realised that the treatments in common use were not just useless, but often outright dangerous. Their criticism of *heroic medicine* led to crucial reforms and helped to improve health care for the benefit of millions.

Homeopaths also introduced the concept of testing medicines on healthy volunteers and initiated research methodologies like the *placebo*-controlled trial, which are the bedrock of medical research today.

2. There Are No Plausible Theories to Explain Homeopathy

There are several *theories* which might go some way to explaining how homeopathy works. As mentioned above, these are currently just theories, and none provides a full explanation of the *mechanism of action* of highly *diluted* remedies. Yet, to claim that homeopathy is totally implausible might be an exaggeration. Moreover, not all homeopathic remedies are highly diluted and thus some can contain pharmacologically active compounds for affecting human health; they cannot therefore be classified as implausible.

3. There Is No Credible Evidence at all that Supports Homeopathy

Several well-conducted *clinical studies* of homeopathy with positive results have been published. It is therefore not true to claim that there is no good trial *evidence* at all.

4. All Homeopaths Are Charlatans Who Have Nothing to Offer to Their Patients

A *charlatan* is a person who falsely pretends to know or be something in order to deceive people. It would be wrong to claim that all homeopaths aim at deceiving their patients. And it would be misleading to say that homeopaths have nothing to offer to their patients. Many patients of homeopaths primarily treasure the long and *compassionate* consultations that homeopaths usually have with their patients and see the homeopathic remedy as secondary.

5. Patients Who Use Homeopathy Must Be Stupid

It would be arrogant, insulting, and counter-productive to *claim* that everyone who uses homeopathy is stupid. Patients consult homeopaths mostly because they have needs which are not met by conventional medicine, but which they feel are taken care of by homeopathy. Seen from this perspective, the use of homeopathy is a poignant criticism of conventional medicine. To dismiss it as stupidity means missing a chance to learn a lesson and to improve mainstream health care.

6. The Assumptions of Homeopathy Are Being Treated like Dogmas

A dogma can be defined as a set of ideas that is considered to be authoritative and accepted uncritically. It is not true that all homeopaths uncritically accept the dictum of Hahnemann. Many, for instance, reject his *miasm* theory of disease, and most combine homeopathic with conventional medicines when necessary.

7. Homeopathy Is a Cult

A cult consists of an exclusive group of persons sharing an esoteric interest. Homeopaths do not form a uniform group and they are not truly exclusive; anyone who wants to can join.

Part II
Lexicon of Homeopathy

Chapter 11
Lexicon of Homeopathy

Aggravation

Homeopathic aggravations—Hahnemann called then "an exaltation of the drug symptoms over the analogous disease symptoms"—can be crucial for understanding the basic assumptions of homeopathy. It therefore deserves more detail than most other entries here.

Homeopathic remedies are based on the *like cures like principle*. This means they are, according to homeopathic teaching, capable of causing the very symptoms which *homeopaths* want to cure. Homeopaths therefore expect that, by administering the optimal remedy to patients, their symptoms will worsen. They believe that this drug-induced reaction—they call it an *artificial disease*—activates the body's healing mechanisms and so brings about the cure.

Homeopaths expect *aggravations* in most of their patients but, frequently, the aggravation may not be noticeable because the symptoms of the disease and the aggravation are identical. Hahnemann wrote:

> [...] even the very smallest dose of a homeopathic remedy always causes a small homeopathic aggravation. [...] this aggravation so closely resembles the original disease that it seems to the patient to be a real worsening of his symptoms.

In about one quarter of cases, homeopaths predict these effects to be strong enough to be clinically verifiable.

Aggravations are thought to last between several hours and a few days. Homeopaths consider them not to be side-effects of their remedies; Hahnemann saw them as "a very good prognostic sign", indicating that the optimal remedy had been administered and a cure would ensue.

The question whether homeopathic aggravations are fact or fiction has been investigated by evaluating the *evidence* from all the *placebo*-controlled *clinical trials* which reported aggravations. Thus it was possible to check whether such reactions occurred more frequently in patients who had taken homeopathic remedies than in

© Springer International Publishing Switzerland 2016
E. Ernst, *Homeopathy - The Undiluted Facts*,
DOI 10.1007/978-3-319-43592-3_11

patients who had been given placebos. The results of this evaluation showed that the perception of an aggravation was as frequent after homeopathic treatments as after placebos.

Nonetheless, most homeopaths continue to believe in the existence of aggravations, a belief that can have serious consequences: some homeopaths might tell their patients that a worsening of their symptoms after taking a homeopathic remedy is a good sign, an assumption which can, in extreme cases, endanger life.

Agrohomeopathy

Agrohomeopathy is a somewhat exotic fringe area of homeopathy. It is the term describing the use of homeopathic remedies to treat gardens and crops. Its proponents claim that it is an *effective*, chemical free, non-toxic method of growing plants. They also believe that agrohomeopathy renders plants resistant to disease by strengthening them 'from the inside out'. Agrohomeopathy, they say, can even treat a trauma retained in the 'biological memory' of the plant, resulting from conditions such as forced hybridization, moving to places outside their natural habitats, or exaggerated fertilization. There is no *evidence*, however, that any of these assumptions are correct.

Allopathy

Allopathy is a term coined by *Hahnemann* for conventional medicine in order to differentiate the two. Allopathic treatments bear no relation to the nature of the symptoms they aim to cure. Originally, allopathy was meant as a derogatory term, but it nevertheless became commonly used and has today almost entirely lost its negative connotation. In Germany, for instance, most pharmacies display large signs 'Allopathy Homeopathy' to signify that they sell both conventional medicines and homeopathic remedies.

Alternative Medicine

Alternative medicine is a commonly used umbrella term for treatments and diagnostic methods which are used by alternative practitioners, but not normally employed by conventional physicians, and which adhere to different principles than conventional medicine. Popular types of alternative medicine include acupuncture, *herbal medicine*, chiropractic, aromatherapy, *naturopathy*, and of course homeopathy.

Numerous synonymous or overlapping terms exist, for instance, complementary medicine or integrative medicine. In most parts of the world, alternative medicine has become increasingly popular during the last 50 years or so. In many countries, homeopathy is amongst the most widely-used forms of alternative medicine.

Contrary to what the word 'alternative' implies, the vast majority of patients employ these treatments in parallel with conventional health care. However, *Hahnemann* was very clear that homeopathic remedies must never be combined with conventional drugs. Despite his strict instructions, most practitioners today use homeopathy alongside conventional medicines (Fig. 11.1).

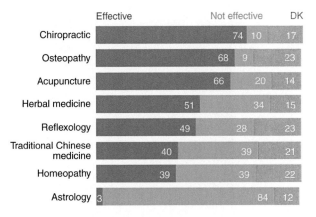

Fig. 11.1 Views on alternative medicine in Britain in 2015

Animal Studies

In conventional medicine, studies on animals are often necessary to test the effects of drugs. In homeopathy, animal studies are sometimes used to determine whether homeopathic remedies have effects beyond *placebo*. Many proponents claim that homeopathic remedies are better than placebos because animal studies prove this to be true. However, this argument is misleading: the most recent *systematic review* of animal studies of homeopathy found that there is only

> [...] very limited evidence that clinical intervention in animals using homeopathic medicines is distinguishable from corresponding intervention using placebos. The low number and quality of the trials hinders a more decisive conclusion.

Anthroposophic Medicine

Anthroposophic medicine is a form of health care which was inspired by homeopathy. Developed in the 1920s by Rudolf *Steiner* (1861–1925) in conjunction with Ita Wegman (1876–1943), anthroposophic medicine is based on more general, occult notions and mystical concepts which Steiner called 'anthroposophy'. For instance, proponents of anthroposophic medicine assume that our past lives influence our present health, and that the course of an illness is determined by our 'karmic' destiny (Fig. 11.2).

Today, anthroposophic medicine is popular, particularly in German-speaking countries, and it has recently also spread to other parts of the world. Practitioners of anthroposophic medicine are usually medical doctors who employ a variety of treatment techniques including massage, exercise, counselling, and a range of remedies. Most of these are, like homeopathic remedies, highly *diluted*, but they are not normally prescribed according to the *like cures like principle*, and are therefore distinct from homeopathy.

Fig. 11.2 Rudolf Steiner
(1861–1925), founder of
anthroposophic medicine

The most widely used anthroposophic remedy is currently a fermented mistletoe extract promoted for cancer and commercially available as 'Iscador'. Steiner argued that the mistletoe plant grows parasitically on a tree and eventually kills it—just as a malignant tumor grows in a body and may kill it; therefore, he reckoned this extract was a cure for cancer.

Anthroposophic medicine is not supported by sound *evidence*. Its treatments are mostly harmless but practitioners may nevertheless cause harm. For instance, they tend to advise against *immunizations*, and this can of course have detrimental effects on individuals as well as on the societal level.

Arndt–Schulz Law

The Arndt–Schulz law depicts the phenomenon that low concentration of some drugs can stimulate biological systems, while high concentrations inhibit them. It was discovered in the 1880s by Dr. H.R. Arndt and Prof H. Schulz from the University of Greifswald, Germany. More recently the phenomenon became known in pharmacology as *hormesis*.

Homeopaths claim that the Arndt–Schulz law explains the *like cures like principle* of homeopathy: a homeopathic remedy causes a symptom at a high concentration which, at a low concentration, it is supposed to cure. Critics, however, point out that such bi-phasic or hermetic responses can be observed with some, but by no means all substances. Therefore, hormesis cannot be used to explain homeopathy, where such a response is claimed for all materials and is considered to be a *law* of nature. Moreover, most homeopathic remedies do not contain low concentrations, but in fact no concentration of active molecules at all, and this further invalidates the theory that this law might explain homeopathy's *mechanism of action*.

Arnica

Homeopaths use thousands of different remedies and, in this book, I will discuss only a few of these which, for one reason or another, have special significance. Arnica

Fig. 11.3 Arnica, drawn by Franz Eugen Köhler, Köhler's Medizinal-Pflanzen

is important simply because it is one of the best known and most popular of all homeopathic remedies.

Homeopathic Arnica is made from Arnica montana, a toxic perennial herbaceous plant, which grows abundantly in the Alps and many other mountain ranges world-wide. Homeopathic Arnica remedies must not be confused with *herbal* preparations of the same plant. The latter are poisonous, if taken by mouth, and therefore only for external use.

Homeopathic Arnica products are highly *diluted*; therefore, they are non-toxic and can be used for both external and internal administration. Homeopathic arnica is used mostly in *clinical homeopathy*; that is to say it is employed by clinicians and patients—it is readily available as an OTC product—for 'cuts and bruises', without the need to account for the individual characteristics of the patient.

Several *clinical trials* have tested whether homeopathic Arnica is better than placebo for healing injuries. Two independent *systematic reviews* evaluating the totality of this *evidence* have cast serious doubt on its *effectiveness* (Fig. 11.3).

Arsenic

Arsenic is a popular homeopathic remedy. Pure arsenic is, of course, extremely toxic; homeopathic remedies of arsenic are, however, given in *high potencies* which usually no longer contain a single molecule of arsenic.

Artificial Disease

Homeopaths claim that the administration of a homeopathic remedy will cause a set of symptoms in a healthy person. This set of symptoms is called an artificial disease and corresponds to the *drug picture* that emerged in *provings* of the same remedy.

When a patient suffering from a set of symptoms receives the optimal remedy (that is, the remedy which causes a very similar set of symptoms when given to a healthy volunteer in a proving), the artificial disease matching his symptoms would initially slightly worsen the patient's condition, a phenomenon called homeopathic *aggravation*. The artificial disease is supposed to stimulate the body's *vital force* which, in turn, gains enough strength to eliminate the original disease that is being treated. According to the teaching of homeopathy, the artificial disease is therefore part of the curative response to the administration of the correct homeopathic remedy.

Avogadro's Number

Amedeo Avogadro (1776–1856), an Italian professor of mathematical physics, for-mulated the theory that, under identical conditions, equal volumes of all gases contain the same number of molecules. Other physicists, such as Johan Joseph Loschmidt (1821–1895) and Jean Baptiste Perrin (1870–1942), used his insights to calcu-late the number of molecules present in one mole of a substance; this number is $6.022\,141\,29(27) \times 10^{23}\ \mathrm{mol}^{-1}$. It is today known as Avogadro's number (Fig. 11.4).

Fig. 11.4 Lorenzo Romano Amedeo Carlo Avogadro di Quaregna e di Cerreto (1776–1856)

This knowledge allows one to calculate the *dilution* or *potency* at which a homeo-pathic remedy no longer is likely to contain a single molecule of the *mother tincture*. Early homeopaths, including *Hahnemann*, were not aware of Avogadro's work. In the *Organon*, Hahnemann nevertheless anticipated its relevance:

> The doctrine of the divisibility of matter teaches us that we cannot make a part so small that it shall cease to be something, and that it shall not share all the properties of the whole.

Homeopathic remedies which are diluted beyond Avogadro's number (D23 or C12 potencies) are often called *ultra-molecular*. Critics of homeopathy point out that, because such remedies are devoid of active molecules, they cannot possibly have health effects.

Bach Flower Remedies

Homeopathy has inspired several innovators to create their very own treatments based on concepts close to but not identical with those of *Hahnemann*. Perhaps the most famous of these was Edward Bach (1886–1936). Bach, a physician and bacteriologist, conducted research on bacterial *vaccines* and, in 1920, took up a post at the *Royal London Homeopathic Hospital*, where he modified his vaccines according to homeopathic principles and called them bowel *nosodes*.

In the late 1920s, he began to view disease from a spiritual perspective and attempted to develop his intuition in order to sense the healing properties of plants. This led him to give up his job, leaving London and moving to rural Wales to develop his 38 flower remedies.

Bach came to believe that early morning sunlight passing through dew drops on flower petals transferred healing energy from the flowers into the water. He would collect the dew drops from the plants and preserve them in brandy to produce a stock for further *dilution*. Later, he modified this technique, suspending flowers in spring water and allowing the sun to shine on them to generate his stock. Today, Bach flower remedies are prepared either by placing the sunlit flowers into pure water, or for more robust plants, by boiling flowers on their twigs in pure water. There is no further dilution and no *succussion*.

Bach viewed illness as the result of a conflict between the purposes of the soul and the personality's actions. This internal conflict was, according to Bach, the cause of emotional imbalances and energetic blockages, which generated a lack of harmony, thus leading to physical diseases. Bach wrote that:

> [...] disease will never be cured or eradicated by present materialistic methods, for the simple reason that disease in its origin is not material [...] Disease is in essence the result of conflict between the Soul and Mind and will never be eradicated except by spiritual and mental effort.

Bach flower remedies are prescribed according to the patient's emotional characteristics and response to illness. Each of his 38 remedies is thought to have unique associations with specific psychological states, which are seen as the main causes of illness.

Bach flower remedies have in common with homeopathic remedies that they are highly diluted, and that they are claimed to work, not through their pharmacological effects, but via 'subtle energies'. The full list of Bach's remedies and the associated emotional states is as follows:

- Agrimony. Mental torture behind a cheerful face.
- Aspen. Fear of unknown things.
- Beech. Intolerance.
- Centaury. The inability to say 'no'.
- Cerato. Lack of trust in one's own decisions.
- Cherry plum. Fear of the mind giving way.
- Chestnut bud. Failure to learn from mistakes.
- Chicory. Selfish, possessive love.
- Clematis. Dreaming of the future without working in the present.
- Crab apple. The cleansing remedy, also for self-hatred.
- Elm. Overwhelmed by responsibility.
- Gentian. Discouragement after a setback.
- Gorse. Hopelessness and despair.
- Heather. Self-centredness and self-concern.

- Holly. Hatred, envy, and jealousy.
- Honeysuckle. Living in the past.
- Hornbeam. Procrastination, tiredness at the thought of doing something.
- Impatiens. Impatience.
- Larch. Lack of confidence.
- Mimulus. Fear of known things.
- Mustard. Deep gloom for no reason.
- Oak. The plodder who keeps going past the point of exhaustion.
- Olive. Exhaustion following mental or physical effort.
- Pine. Guilt.
- Red chestnut. Over-concern for the welfare of loved ones.
- Rock rose. Terror and fright.
- Rock Water. Self-denial, rigidity, and self-repression.
- Scleranthus. Inability to choose between alternatives.
- Star of Bethlehem. Shock.
- Sweet chestnut. Extreme mental anguish, when everything has been tried and there is no light left.
- Vervain. Over-enthusiasm.
- Vine. Dominance and inflexibility.
- Walnut. Protection from change and unwanted influences.
- Water violet. Pride and aloofness.
- White chestnut. Unwanted thoughts and mental arguments.
- Wild oat. Uncertainty over one's direction in life.
- Wild rose. Drifting, resignation, and apathy.
- Willow. Self-pity and resentment.
- Rescue remedy. A combination remedy made up of five different remedies, promoted to counter anxiety and stress.

In recent years, other 'flower remedies' have been added to this original list. However, only the original 38 remedies are allowed to carry the name 'Bach'.

Bans on Homeopathy

In the 19th century, homeopathy got banned in several countries. This was mainly due to the strong opposition and influence of physicians and pharmacists. In Austria, for instance, the Kaiser issued a decree on 19 October 1819 that "Dr. Hahnemann's homeopathic healing method be generally and strictly forbidden". Few homeopaths dared to practice in the Austrian–Hungarian Empire during the ban, but it was lifted on 2 February 1837.

Basic Research

Basic research in homeopathy may involve testing the effects of homeopathy in test tubes or on animals. These tests might aim to determine whether homeopathy is effective in the chosen model. The results of such investigations have been reviewed by A. Vickers, and his conclusion was that:

[…] there is a lack of independent replication of any pre-clinical research in homoeopathy. In the few instances where a research team has set out to replicate the work of another, either the results were negative or the methodology was questionable.

Basic research in homeopathy can also mean the investigation of possible *mechanisms of action* of homeopathic remedies. In this context, numerous avenues have been explored and the science behind them is often complex. A comprehensive summary was published in 2007 in an entire issue of the journal Homeopathy. An independent team of scientists from Ars Technica published a most thorough evaluation of these articles [http://arstechnica.com/science/2007/09/the-pseudoscience-behind-homeopathy/1/]. Their conclusions seem important enough to be quoted here in full:

[…] the homeopathic community has consistently demanded that their practice be viewed as scientific, presumably to obtain the credibility that traditional medicine receives. As our article reveals, they hope to achieve this without actually engaging in scientific practices. In doing so, they have adopted many of the techniques used in other fields of pseudoscience:

- Ignore settled issues in science: We know a great deal about the behavior of water (and evolution, and other contentious topics), but there are many efforts to introduce new science without ever addressing the existing body of knowledge. As such, many of the basic tenets of topics such as homeopathy appear to be ungrounded in reality as we understand it.

- Misapplication of real science: Quantum mechanics is an undeniably successful description of parts of the natural world, but the limitations of its applicability are widely recognized by the scientific community, if not the general public. Pseudoscientists such as homeopaths appear to cynically target this sort of ignorance by applying scientific principles to inappropriate topics.

- Rejection of scientific standards: Over the centuries, science has established standards of evidence and experiment to ensure that data remains consistent and reproducible. But these strengths are presented as weaknesses that make science impervious to new ideas, a stance that is often accompanied by:

- Claims of suppression: Pseudoscience is rejected because it does not conform to the standards held by the scientific community. That community is depicted as a dangerous hegemony that rejects new ideas in order to perpetuate a stifling orthodoxy. This happens in spite of many examples of radical ideas that have rapidly gained not only acceptance, but major prizes, when they were properly supported by scientific evidence.

- A conclusion/evidence gap: Many areas of pseudoscience do not set out to examine a phenomenon but rather have the stated goal of supporting a preordained conclusion. As such, they often engage in excessive logical leaps when the actual data is insufficient to support the desired conclusion.

- Focusing on the fringes: All areas of science have anomalous data and anecdotal findings that are inconsistent with the existing understanding. But those anomalies should not obscure the fact that the vast majority of current data does support the predominant theories. In the hands of a pseudoscientist, these unconnected edge cases are presented as a coherent body of knowledge that supports the replacement of existing understandings.

Perhaps the clearest theme running through many areas of pseudoscience, however, is the attempt to make a whole that is far, far greater than the sum of its parts. Enlarging a collection of terminally-flawed trivia does not somehow strengthen its scientific significance. This is especially true when many of the components of the argument don't form a coherent whole. For example, quantum entanglement, structured water, and silica are essentially unrelated explanations, and any support for one of them makes no difference to the others. Yet, somehow, presenting them all at once is supposed to make the case for water's memory harder to dismiss.

Benveniste Affair

Jacques Benveniste (1935–2004) was a French scientist who became famous in the world of homeopathy because, in 1979, he published a paper in the journal Nature about the effects of high dilutions of anti-IgE antibody on the degranulation of human basophils. His results seemed to support the assumption that *ultra-high dilutions* can have biological effects. His findings were, however, discredited by a team of three sceptics who went into his laboratory and demonstrated that the results were due to *bias*; once the source of the bias had been identified and eliminated, the *high dilutions* behaved exactly as a *placebo*. Since then, several replications of his study have been published, the majority of which failed to reproduce Benveniste's original findings.

Berlin Wall

Many consumers believe that homeopathic remedies are always manufactured from plants and other natural *stock*. This is, however, not true, and Berlin wall is a good example of the many remedies produced from man-made materials (Fig. 11.5). Below are just a few of the numerous symptoms and conditions this remedy is currently recommended for:

- Feeling of being forsaken.
- Oppression.
- States of possession.
- Children of ambitious parents who are pushed.

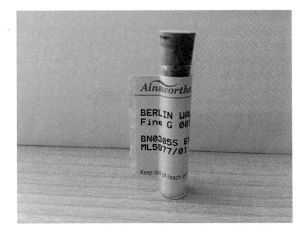

Fig. 11.5 Berlin wall as a commercially available homeopathic remedy. *Photo credit* Simon Singh. 100 ml of the remedy in 'medicating potency' currently costs £64.50 (see www.ainsworths.com/index.php?node= RemedyStore2\&_action= agent.add\&remedy=18379)

- Indescribable evil/darkness.
- Suspicious, uneasy, shifty eyes; cannot look you in the eye.
- Frequent weeping, tears just flow; sense of numbness or despair over them.
- Deep grief which cannot be accessed, unspoken, but which hangs in the air.
- Depression, sense of blackness, total isolation, aloneness, despair.
- Panic.
- Deceit.

Bias

Bias is the term used to describe a systematic deviation from the truth. In research, bias has the power to produce results that are wrong or misleading. In studies of homeopathy, bias tends to generate false-positive results. The most important types of bias in this context are publication bias and selection bias. The former describes the tendency that positive results get published, while negative findings remain unpublished, a phenomenon that will inevitably generate a false-positive overall picture, for instance, when conducting *systematic reviews*. Selection bias is an inherent limitation of clinical trials where the allocation of patients to two treatments, for instance homeopathy and a conventional drug, is by choice of the patient or the physician. The consequence can be that those patients expecting benefit from homeopathy chose homeopathy and those that don't chose the conventional drug. In turn, these *expectations* would have a powerful influence on the outcome. Such selection bias is best eliminated through randomised allocation to treatment groups.

In the practice of homeopathy, recall bias often causes a deviation from the truth. Clinicians tend to remember their therapeutic successes, while forgetting their failures. Over time, this will generate a false-positive impression about the *effectiveness* of homeopathy.

Bier, August

Professor Bier (1861–1949) was a prominent and innovative German surgeon who, towards the end of his career, started sympathising with homeopathy. He founded the Society for the Examination of Homeopathic Drugs and, in 1925, he published an article entitled Wie sollen wir uns zur Homeopathie stellen? (How should we look upon homeopathy?) It triggered a flurry of interest in homeopathy but brought Bier harsh criticism from his mainstream colleagues. The Nazis were keen on homeopathy and took advantage of Bier and his views, even though Bier himself was not a Nazi (Fig. 11.6).

Blackie, Margery Grace

Doctor Blackie (1898–1981) was a British physician and prominent homeopath. She served as a consultant at the *Royal London Homeopathic Hospital*, dean of the UK *Faculty of Homeopathy* (1964–1979), *homeopath* to the Queen, and founder of the

Fig. 11.6 The German
surgeon August Karl Gustav
Bier (1861–1949)

Blackie Foundation Trust. Blackie's only book is entitled The Patient not the Cure.
British homeopaths have created the Blackie Memorial Lecture series in her honour.

Bönninghausen, Clemens Maria Franz von

Bönninghausen (1785–1864) was a Dutch lawyer who became an influential *lay
homeopath* after being cured from tuberculosis with homeopathy in 1828. He wrote
one of the first *repertories*. His son Carl, also a *homeopath*, married Melanie Hahnemann's daughter, whom Samuel *Hahnemann* had adopted and who had inherited
the sixth (and at the time unpublished) edition of the *Organon*, which was published
only in 1921, long after Hahnemann's death (Fig. 11.7).

Boericke, William

Doctor Boericke (1849–1929) was born in Austria where he also began his medical
studies, although he eventually finished them in Philadelphia. He became a leading
figure in US homeopathy and was the founder of a US-based homeopathic *pharmacy*,
which became highly successful. Together with Hahnemann's biographer Richard
Haehl, he successfully negotiated with the *Bönninghausen* family to publish the sixth
edition of the *Organon*, long after *Hahnemann* had died (Fig. 11.8).

Fig. 11.7 Clemens Maria
Franz (Friedrich) Freiherr
(Baron) von Bönninghausen
(1785–1864)

Fig. 11.8 Homeopathic
remedy Rhus toxicodendron,
derived from poison ivy,
produced by Boericke and
Tafel

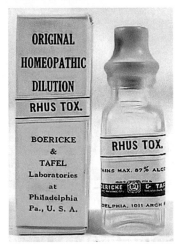

Boiron, Henri and Jean

The twin brothers Henri and Jean Boiron founded Laboratoires Boiron in Lyon,
France, and it has now become the world's largest manufacturer of homeopathic
remedies. One of their best-selling products is Oscillococcinum, which is produced
from duck liver and heart potentised to ultra-molecular dilution. In 1965, the Boirons
succeeded in getting homeopathic remedies included in the French pharmacopeia.
Today, Christian Boiron is the general manager of the firm; when interviewed in
2015 about the recent NHMRC report, he said:

Il y a un Ku Klux Klan contre l'homéopathie [There is a Ku Klux Klan against homeopathy].

Bonneval, Count Henri de

Count Henri de Bonneval (1806–1882) was one of the first to introduce homeopathy to France. Born in Bordeaux as the descendent of an ancient noble family, he became interested in homeopathy and decided to travel to Koethen in order to learn homeopathy directly from *Hahnemann*. Later, in Montpellier, he defended the first French medical thesis devoted to homeopathy and subsequently opened consulting rooms in Bordeaux. Bonneval rapidly gained a solid reputation and a large clientele. At the end of his life, he published a book which introduced homeopathy to the French people.

C30 Potency

This *potency* was Hahnemann's favorite during much of his life. He described his method of preparing a C30 remedy from a herbal *stock* as follows:

> To obtain the hundredth degree of potency, mix two drops of alcohol with equal parts of the juice of the plant, and then mix this with one hundred drops of alcohol, by means of two strokes with the arm from above downwards; by mixing in the same way one drop of this dilution with one hundred drops of alcohol, you obtain the ten thousandth degree of potency, and by mixing a drop of this last dilution with another one hundred drops of alcohol you obtain the millionth degree. This process of spiritualisation or dynamization is continued through a series of thirty phials up to the thirtieth solution. This thirtieth degree should always be used in homeopathic purposes.

Today, the C30 potency is the one most frequently sold over the counter to consumers. A C30 potency is *ultra-molecular*. A single molecule of the substance named on the remedy's label inside a sphere of water with a diameter of 150 million kilometers— the average distance from Earth to the Sun, and an eight-minute journey at the speed of light—would be the equivalent of a C30 potency.

Carstens Stiftung

The Karl und Veronica Carstens Stiftung is a German charity set up in 1882 by the former German President and his wife. Its purpose is to promote the use of *alternative medicine*, and it is the most influential German charity in this sector. The charity has spent millions on research into homeopathy, and more than 600 publications, including over 50 books, have been published as a result. Much of this work has been criticised for being biased and of poor quality.

Case Report

A case report is a document that outlines all the essential details of one single patient's history, signs, symptoms, diagnosis, treatment, *outcome*, and prognosis. Such reports can be valuable in alerting us to certain aspects or possibilities of clinical practice. However, they can never constitute proof of *effectiveness* or establish relations of cause and effect between the treatment and the outcome. In homeopathy, case reports are much-used tools, for instance, for teaching purposes.

Case Series

A case series is a document describing several case reports. The cases normally have some important aspect in common. For instance, they could be describing patients who all had the same symptoms or who all received the same treatment.

Celebrities

Homeopathy has always been supported by people from all levels of society, naturally this also includes the rich and famous. During its early years, for instance, many aristocrats were attracted to it. Today they are joined by numerous other celebrities, including David Beckham, Catherine Zeta-Jones, Usain Bolt, Pamela Anderson, Paul McCartney, Twiggy, Roger Daltrey, Caprice, Susan Hampshire, Tina Turner, Louise Jameson, Gaby Roslin, Jude Law, Sadie Frost, Nadia Sawalha, Richard Branson, Debra Stephenson, Meera Syal, *Prince Charles*, and many more. Some of these individuals regularly speak out publicly in favour of homeopathy, and entire websites as well as books are dedicated to this issue implying that, if they use homeopathy, it must be good. What seems like a reasonable argument to some, however, turns out to be a logical *fallacy*.

Centesimal Potency Scale

The centesimal potency scale relies on *serial dilutions* at the ratio of 1:100 which are performed by adding one part of the previous dilution to 99 parts of diluent and subsequent *succussion*, i.e., vigorous shaking, of the remedy. The remedy is designated by a C and a number which defines the number of serial dilutions. Thus a C30, one of the most commonly used *potencies*, depicts a remedy which has been diluted thirty times at a ratio of 1:100, with succussion at each *dilution* step.

Charges

Today, the first consultation with a *homeopath* usually lasts from 60 to 90 min. Medical homeopaths charge between $150.00 and $500.00. Follow-up visits typically last between 15 and 45 min, and the fees are proportionally less. Most homeopathic remedies are relatively inexpensive; they cost between $5.00 and $20.00.

Charlatan

A charlatan is defined as a person who falsely pretends to know something or be something in order to deceive people. With some simplification and a touch of satire, two types of charlatans can usually be differentiated, but there can, of course, be plenty of overlap between these categories. The dishonest charlatan is the one we usually think of first. Apart from being dishonest, he has a range further characteristics:

- he is relatively rational,
- he knows about *evidence*,
- he is mainly interested in himself,
- he aims to make money,
- he does not believe in his own 'message',
- he does not live by his own rules,
- he is cynical,
- his 'charisma', if he has any, is well-studied and extensively rehearsed,
- when challenged, he sues.

The fantasist charlatan is very different and can be described as follows:

- she is convinced that she is honest,
- she is deluded,
- she ignores the evidence and argues that science is just one of several ways of knowing,
- she feels altruistic,
- she thinks she stands on the moral high ground,
- she is not primarily out to make money,
- she is convinced of the correctness of her message,
- she adheres to her own gospel,
- she abhors cynicism,
- her charisma, if she has any, is real, and a powerful tool for convincing followers,
- when challenged, she feels hurt and misunderstood.

Cherry-Picking

Cherry-picking is the term often used for using *evidence* selectively according to the direction of the result. Thus some homeopaths select the positive trials of homeopathy in an attempt to convince others of the value of homeopathy. Cherry-picking is a sign of *pseudoscience* or even fraud. The correct way to present evidence is on the basis of all the available and reliable data.

Chiropractor

Many chiropractors employ a range of treatments, including homeopathy, particularly those in the USA. Their understanding of medicine often seems bizarre. A good example is this recent quote from an American chiropractor:

> Homeopathy can be the perfect complement to chiropractic care. It can correct the energetics (including the genetics) of the deepest areas of the body, mind, and emotions, where the hands of the chiropractor can't reach.

Cinchona

See *quinine*.

Claims by Proponents of Homeopathy

Hahnemann postulated that homeopathy can cure any symptoms which can affect humans. He believed that the nature of a disease cannot be known and was therefore not interested in disease labels. Many *homeopaths* still adhere to these ideas; they claim to treat the individual patient and not the disease. Since they treat the *individual* patient regardless of what he or she may be suffering from, it can be assumed that they treat all diseases which afflict mankind.

Some homeopaths thus extrapolate that homeopathy is *effective* regardless of the disease someone is suffering from. Put differently, this suggests to some homeopaths that they are able to treat all human diseases. Consequently, we find therapeutic claims by homeopaths and their supporters for every condition imaginable. They range from common benign diseases such as eczema or arthritis to serious diseases like cancer or AIDS, from rare infections like *Ebola* to personal idiosyncrasies such as *homosexuality*.

Class Actions

In recent years, several class action suits have been filed in North America against manufacturers of homeopathic products. One of the first of these cases was filed in 2011 in the Superior Court of California against the homeopathic manufacturer *Boiron*. The company had allegedly violated consumer protection laws by falsely advertising and selling *Oscillococcinum*. It was alleged that this product is merely a sugar pill, and has no impact on influenza or accompanying symptoms. The plaintiffs claimed that the probability of getting one molecule of active ingredient of Oscillo-coccinum in a regular dosage is approximately equivalent to winning the Powerball lottery every week for an entire year. Boiron set aside $5M to settle the claims, and the company stated that:

> [...] at the end of the day consumers need additional information that we're happy to provide.

It is estimated that this class action cost Boiron around $7 million.

Classical Homeopathy

Classical homeopathy is the term used to describe the type of homeopathy that adheres to the principles, instructions, and methods published by *Hahnemann*. As Hahnemann's texts are by no means free of contradictions, classical homeopathy is not a well-defined concept. As it is practised today, it incorporates ideas that originate not from Hahnemann but also from other prominent homeopaths, such as *Kent*.

Thus some might use the term 'classical homeopathy' to denote the highly *individualised* prescribing of Hahnemann and to contrast it with the symptom-orientated prescribing of *clinical homeopathy*. Others might employ it to distinguish those *homeopaths* who would practise no method other than homeopathy from those who regularly combine homeopathy with conventional medicine. Others again might take it to mean *unicist* homeopathy, administering a single remedy at a time, as Hahnemann generally did.

Clergy

From its early days, homeopathy has attracted clergymen, and extensive homeopathic activities of clerical healers and missionaries are well documented. The attraction of clergymen to homeopathy seems understandable in view of the relatively easy acquisition of basic homeopathic skills and homeopathy's emphasis on the *individuality* of the patient and the spiritual dimension of healing. Homeopathy enabled the clergy to counter the prevailing 'mechanistic' and 'materialistic' trends in conventional medicine. Some clergymen also combined homeopathy with religious healing methods.

Clinical Homeopathy

While *classical homeopathy* relies on *individualised* prescribing according to the *like cures like principle* and selects the optimal remedy for each patient based on the findings from *provings*, clinical homeopathy more closely resembles the way drugs are prescribed in conventional medicine; it selects the appropriate remedy according to the condition of the patient, while largely disregarding the like cure like principle.

However, clinical and classical homeopathy are not mutually exclusive; in fact, there is considerable overlap between the two approaches, and they are often used in parallel by the same clinician. In other words, if the symptoms of a patient reveal a very clear indication for a certain homeopathic remedy, clinical homeopathy is used even by classical *homeopaths*. For instance, *Arnica* is considered a clear indication for cuts and bruises, as is Coffea for insomnia, Drosera for coughs, Opium for constipation, and so on, and these remedies would be employed regularly by classical homeopaths.

Clinical homeopathy is also used by many non-homeopaths as well as by consumers when they self-prescribe. It does not require any understanding of the principles of homeopathy, nor its finer details. Moreover, clinical homeopathy is also the predominant approach in *veterinary homeopathy*.

Clinical Trial

The *effectiveness* or *efficacy* of treatments such as homeopathy are best verified in clinical trials. In essence, these are experiments where a group of patients is typically divided into two subgroups. One subgroup receives the experimental therapy, e.g., homeopathy, while the other subgroup, the control group, gets a different treatment. At the end of the treatment period, the *outcomes* for each group are documented and compared. Depending on the exact research question, the control group might receive:

- a *placebo*,
- no therapy at all,
- a therapy that is known to work for the condition in question.

There are dozens of variations of this basic design of a clinical trial. The total group of patients can be divided into subgroups according to a random code; this would ensure that the two groups are comparable even in characteristics that cannot be quantified. Similarly the patients and investigators can be left in the dark as to who receives which form of treatment; such trials are said to be single or double blind. Both these design features reduce the risk of *bias*, i.e., the chances that the result is reliable are increased.

The study design that leaves the least room for bias is the placebo-controlled, double-blind, randomised clinical trial. In such a study, patients are randomised into two groups; the control group receives a placebo which should be indistinguishable from the experimental treatment, and neither the patients nor the researchers can tell which patient is being treated with which of the two treatment options. Thus the results of the study are independent of both the *expectation* of a particular outcome and placebo effects.

Some argue that homeopathy is too subtle, holistic, and individualised to be squeezed into the 'straight-jacket' of such a rigorous test. This notion is, however, based on a misunderstanding. Hundreds of placebo-controlled, double-blind, randomised clinical trials of homeopathy have been conducted, and many take full account of the subtle, holistic, and individualised nature of homeopathy.

Cochrane Collaboration, Cochrane Reviews

The Cochrane Collaboration is a worldwide organisation of researchers who agree that systematic reviews are important for making the best possible therapeutic decisions. Their aim is to help others by publishing *systematic reviews* of the highest quality and keeping them up-to-date. Cochrane reviews tend to be transparent and devoid of *bias*, and they are freely available on the Internet for anyone who wants to read them.

To date, 8 Cochrane reviews of homeopathy have been published for 8 different conditions. All have been conducted with the cooperation of experienced *homeopaths*. Their conclusions are as follows.

Irritable Bowel Syndrome [http://www.ncbi.nlm.nih.gov/pubmed/24222383]

A pooled analysis of two small studies suggests a possible benefit for clinical homeopathy, using the remedy asafoetida, over placebo for people with constipation-predominant IBS. These results should be interpreted with caution due to the low quality of reporting in these trials, high or unknown risk of bias, short-term follow-up, and sparse data. One small study found no statistical difference between individualised homeopathy and usual care (defined as high doses of dicyclomine hydrochloride, faecal bulking agents, and diet sheets advising a high fibre diet). No conclusions can be drawn from this study due to the low number of participants and the high risk of bias in this trial. In addition, it is likely that usual care has changed since this trial was conducted. Further high quality, adequately powered RCTs are required to assess the efficacy and safety of clinical and individualised homeopathy compared to placebo or usual care.

Homeopathic Oscillococcinum for Influenza
[http://www.ncbi.nlm.nih.gov/pubmed/23235586]

There is insufficient good evidence to enable robust conclusions to be made about *Oscillococcinum* in the prevention or treatment of influenza and influenza-like illness. Our findings do not rule out the possibility that Oscillococcinum could have a clinically useful treatment effect but, given the low quality of the eligible studies, the evidence is not compelling. There was no evidence of clinically important harms due to Oscillococcinum.

Homeopathy for Psychiatric Disorders
[http://www.ncbi.nlm.nih.gov/pubmed/21733480]

The database on studies of homeopathy and placebo in psychiatry is very limited, but results do not preclude the possibility of some benefit.

Homeopathy for Treating the Side-Effects of Cancer Therapies
[http://www.ncbi.nlm.nih.gov/pubmed/19370613]

This review found preliminary data in support of the efficacy of topical calendula for prophylaxis of acute dermatitis during radiotherapy and Traumeel S mouthwash in the treatment of chemotherapy-induced stomatitis. These trials need replicating. There is no convincing evidence for the efficacy of homeopathic medicines for other adverse effects of cancer treatments. Further research is required.

Homeopathy for Attention Deficit/Hyperactivity Disorder (ADHD)
[http://www.ncbi.nlm.nih.gov/pubmed/17943868]

There is currently little evidence for the efficacy of homeopathy for the treatment of ADHD. Development of optimal treatment protocols is recommended prior to further randomised controlled trials being undertaken.

Homeopathy for Chronic Asthma [http://www.ncbi.nlm.nih.gov/pubmed/14973954]

There is not enough evidence to reliably assess the possible role of homeopathy in asthma. As well as randomised trials, there is a need for observational data to document the different methods of homeopathic prescribing and how patients respond. This will help to establish to what extent people respond to a 'package of care' rather than the homeopathic intervention alone.

Homeopathy for Inducing Labour [http://www.ncbi.nlm.nih.gov/pubmed/14583972]

There is insufficient evidence to recommend the use of homoeopathy as a method of induction. It is likely that the demand for complementary medicine will continue and women will continue to consult a homoeopath during their pregnancy. Although caulophyllum is a commonly used homoeopathic therapy to induce labour, the treatment strategy used in the one trial in which it was evaluated may not reflect routine homoeopathy practice. Rigorous evaluations of individualised homeopathic therapies for induction of labour are needed.

Homeopathy for Dementia [http://www.ncbi.nlm.nih.gov/pubmed/12535487]

In view of the absence of evidence it is not possible to comment on the use of homeopathy in treating dementia. The extent of homeopathic prescribing for people with dementia is not clear and so it is difficult to comment on the importance of conducting trials in this area.

None of these reviews were able to draw a convincingly positive conclusion stating that the best available *evidence* proves homeopathy to be *effective*. In other words, the most reliable evidence available to date fails to support the notion that homeopathy is effective beyond *placebo*.

Commonly Used Remedies

Homeopaths use thousands of different remedies in dozens of different *potencies*. According to the popular website 'abc homeopathy', the most frequently used 36 homeopathic remedies (in order of popularity) are:

1. Sulphur	13. Causticum	25. Baryta Carbonica
2. Arsenicum Album	14. Nux Vomica	26. Alumina
3. Phosphorus	15. Lachesis	27. Kali Carbonicum
4. Calcarea Carbonica	16. Silicea	28. Conium Maculatum
5. Lycopodium Clavatum	17. Nitricum Acidum	29. Hepar Sulphuris Calc
6. Pulsatilla Nigricans	18. Apis Mellifica	30. Aurum Metallicum
7. Graphites	19. Aconitum Napellus	31. Mezereum
8. Sepia	20. Kreosotum	32. Phosphoricum Acidum
9. Rhus Toxicodendron	21. Carbo Vegetabilis	33. China Officinalis
10. Natrum Muriaticum	22. Bryonia Alba	34. Petroleum
11. Mercurius Vivus	23. Agaricus Muscarius	35. Thuja Occidentalis
12. Belladonna	24. Argentum Nitricum	36. Aloe Socotrina

However, this information should be taken with a pinch of salt. While these remedies are certainly commonly employed, it seems difficult, perhaps even impossible, to accurately determine which remedies are used most frequently in by homeopaths across the world.

Compassion

Compassion is the feeling that often arises when one is confronted with another person's suffering and one feels motivated to relieve that suffering. In general, *homeopaths* are known to be very compassionate clinicians, and it is possible that this fact significantly contributes to the benefit many patients experience after consulting a homeopath.

Complex Homeopathy

Complex homeopathy is the use of preparations which contain more than one homeopathic remedy. Even though it is not in line with *Hahnemann's* teachings, complex homeopathy is currently highly popular and commercially successful. Homeopathic combination remedies can be bought over the counter and usually contain a range of different remedies which, according to the concepts of *clinical homeopathy*, are most likely to cure a given condition.

Conditioning

Conditioning, also known as classical or Pavlovian conditioning, is a subconscious learning process in which a certain response to a potent stimulus comes to be elicited in response to a previously neutral stimulus. This is achieved by repeatedly pairing the neutral stimulus with the potent stimulus. Conditioning was discovered by Pavlov who repeatedly rang a bell when feeding dogs, and this thereby came to stimulate the flow of gastric secretions. Having done this for a while, he rang the bell without supplying food and noticed that the dogs' flow of gastric juices was nevertheless stimulated. In other words, Pavlov had conditioned them in such a way that the sound of the bell was now stimulating the flow of gastric secretions.

Conditioning is an important part of the *placebo* response. In medicine, it means that patients will subconsciously learn that consulting a clinician, for instance, is usually followed by symptomatic improvement. Subsequently, a patient may feel better, even if the doctor administered an *ineffective* therapy. It follows that the perceived benefit from a homeopathic prescription might be unrelated to the effect of the remedy itself, but could be due to the patient's conditioning (Fig. 11.9).

Conflicts of Interest

A conflict of interest arises when a person or organization is involved in multiple interests, one of which could possibly corrupt their motivation or objectivity. In health care, we often just focus on financial conflicts of interest, but other conflicts, such as strong beliefs, can be just as powerful. In homeopathy, it is primarily the latter that may cloud the objectivity of proponents.

Confounder

Confounder is a term used in research to describe factors influencing the *outcome* of an experiment or observation other than those factors under investigation. A prominent confounding factor in homeopathy can, for instance, be noted in relation to the apparently superior results obtained with homeopathic treatment in *epidemics* during the early days of homeopathy. They might have been due to confounding by

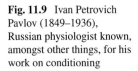

Fig. 11.9 Ivan Petrovich
Pavlov (1849–1936),
Russian physiologist known,
amongst other things, for his
work on conditioning

the detrimental therapies applied in conventional medicine of the time (see *heroic medicine*).

Considerations Before Consulting a Homeopath

The website of the US National Institute of Health lists the following useful considerations for people who are tempted to consult a *homeopath* or to self-medicate with homeopathic remedies:

- Do not use homeopathy as a replacement for proven conventional care or to postpone seeing a health care provider about a medical problem.
- If you are considering using a homeopathic remedy, bring the product with you when you visit your health care provider. The provider may be able to help you determine whether the product might pose a risk of side effects or drug interactions.
- Follow the recommended conventional immunization schedules for children and adults. Do not use homeopathic products as a substitute for conventional immunizations.

- Women who are pregnant or nursing, or people who are thinking of using home-opathy to treat a child, should consult their (or their child's) health care providers.
- Tell all your health care providers about any complementary health practices you use. Give them a full picture of all you do to manage your health. This will ensure coordinated and safe care.

Constitution

In homeopathy, constitution describes the pattern of characteristics of an individual patient. These can be of a physical or psychological nature or refer to reactions to stimuli and everyday circumstances. The constitution of an individual is often believed to remain constant throughout his or her life.

The concept of constitution led to 'constitutional prescribing', which denotes the prescription of homeopathic remedies according to a patient's constitution rather than his or her clinical picture or symptoms. Constitutional remedies are homeopathic preparations that match certain constitutions in patients.

Cost-Effectiveness Analysis

Cost-effectiveness analysis is an *economic evaluation* comparing the relative costs and outcomes of two or more treatments for the same condition. Such assessments are important when deciding which treatments should and which shouldn't be funded from the public purse, for instance. Researchers have not identified a single disease or condition for which homeopathy would appear to be more cost-effective than the appropriate conventional treatment.

Critical Analysis

Critical analysis is a process for making decisions based on (often confusing) *evidence*. According to the National Council for Excellence in Critical Thinking it is the intellectually disciplined process of actively and skillfully conceptualizing, applying, analyzing, synthesizing, and/or evaluating information gathered from, or generated by, observation, experience, reflection, reasoning, or communication, as a guide to belief and action.

Carl Sagan explained this superbly:

It seems to me what is called for is an exquisite balance between two conflicting needs: the most skeptical scrutiny of all hypotheses that are served up to us and at the same time a great openness to new ideas. Obviously those two modes of thought are in some tension. But if you are able to exercise only one of these modes, whichever one it is, you're in deep trouble. If you are only skeptical, then no new ideas make it through to you. You never learn anything new. You become a crotchety old person convinced that nonsense is ruling the world. (There is, of course, much data to support you.) But every now and then, maybe once in a hundred cases, a new idea turns out to be on the mark, valid and wonderful. If you are too much in the habit of being skeptical about everything, you are going to miss or resent it, and either way you will be standing in the way of understanding and progress. On the other hand, if you are open to the point of gullibility and have not an ounce of skeptical sense in you, then you cannot distinguish the useful ideas from the worthless ones.

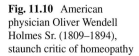

Fig. 11.10 American physician Oliver Wendell Holmes Sr. (1809–1894), staunch critic of homeopathy

Critics of Homeopathy

Homeopathy has been criticized from its early beginnings. Critics mainly focused on two aspects, namely that the assumptions of homeopathy fly in the face of *science* and that the clinical *evidence* fails to show that is *effective* beyond *placebo*.

An example of an early critic of homeopathy is Oliver Wendell Holmes, who famously wrote that homeopathy is (Fig. 11.10):

> [...] a mingled mass of perverse ingenuity, of tinsel erudition, of imbecile credulity, and of artful misinterpretation, too often mingled in practice [...] with heartless and shameless imposition.

In 2015, Alan Schmukler, a prominent US *homeopath*, claimed that:

> [...] there are essentially two categories of critics. The first category consists of individuals who are totally ignorant of homeopathy and just repeating propaganda they've been exposed to. The second category is people who know that homeopathy works, but have a vested financial interest in destroying it.

From this and numerous other indications, it seems that during the last 200 years homeopaths have not been able to address criticism rationally.

Deaths After Homeopathy

Homeopathy is generally assumed to be a *safe* treatment, and this reputation motivates many consumers to try homeopathic treatments. However, this notion might not be entirely correct: numerous deaths after homeopathy have been reported. A website entitled 'What's the harm?', for instance, lists around 30 such fatalities. These tragic incidents are usually directly caused, not by the effects of a homeopathic remedy (in the case of a *low potency* of a toxic substance, this is still a realistic possibility), but rather due to the substitution of homeopathy for an *effective* treatment of a life-threatening condition.

Decimal Potency

Serial dilution at a ratio of 1:10 with *succussion* at each step. See also *potency scales* and *centesimal potency*.

Definitions of Homeopathy

In Chap. 2, we have already seen what is probably the most authorative definition of homeopathy from the *International Dictionary of Homeopathy*:

> Homeopathy is a therapeutic method using substances whose effects, when administered to healthy subjects, correspond to the manifestations of the disorder in the individual patient.

But there are many more, and one could be forgiven for being confused. To provide a flavour, here is a small selection of further definitions:

- Homeopathy is a system of complementary medicine in which ailments are treated by minute doses of natural substances that in larger amounts would produce symptoms of the ailment.
- Homeopathy is a system of alternative medicine created in 1796 by Samuel *Hahnemann* based on his doctrine of *like cures like* (similia similibus curentur), a claim that a substance that causes the symptoms of a disease in healthy people would cure similar symptoms in sick people.
- Homeopathy is the method of treating disease by drugs, given in minute doses, that would produce in a healthy person symptoms similar to those of the disease.
- Homeopathy is a medical science developed by Dr. Samuel Hahnemann (1755–1843), a German physician. It is based on the principle that like cures like. In simple words, it means that any substance which can produce symptoms in a healthy person can cure similar symptoms in a person who is sick.
- Homeopathy is a 'treatment' based on the use of highly *diluted* substances, which practitioners claim can cause the body to heal itself.
- Homeopathy, or homeopathic medicine, is a holistic system of treatment that originated in the late eighteenth century. The name homeopathy is derived from two Greek words that mean 'like disease'. The system is based on the idea that substances that produce symptoms of sickness in healthy people will have a curative effect when given in very dilute quantities to sick people who exhibit those same symptoms.

- A system for treating disease based on the administration of minute doses of a drug that in massive amounts produces symptoms in healthy individuals similar to those of the disease itself.

Dental Homeopathy

Homeopathic dentists have the same dental qualifications as conventional dentists, and are governed by the same *laws* and *regulations*. The difference is that homeopathic dentists employ homeopathy in their regular practice as an additional therapeutic option. In many countries, there exist *professional organisations* for dentists practising homeopathy. The British Homeopathic Dental Association, for instance, *claims* that homeopathic dentists treat patients *holistically*, that their remedies are effective and safe, and that homeopathy can stop swelling or pain and cure conditions such as ulcers and cold sores. However, there is no good *evidence* to support most of these claims.

Detox

Detox stands for detoxification, a term used in conventional medicine for treatments to wean addicts off drugs. In *alternative medicine*, it is a fashionable word for numerous approaches promoted to eliminate toxins from our bodies. Homeopathic remedies are often claimed to be *effective* for that purpose. There is, however, no sound *evidence* that this *claim* is true.

Diluent

In homeopathy, this term describes the *diluting* agent to which *stock* (for instance, a plant extract) is added during *potentisation*. Various materials are used for this purpose. The most common are water, ethanol, and a mixture of water and ethanol. Non-soluble substances are diluted via *trituration*, usually employing *lactose* as the diluent.

Dilution

The manufacturing process of homeopathic remedies normally includes a process of *serial dilution*. At each step, one drop of the previous *potency* is added to 9 (*decimal potency* scale) or 99 (*centesimal potency* scale) of *diluent* prior to *succussion* to produce the subsequent potency. Contrary to *science* where dilution demonstrably leads to a loss of power, in homeopathy, dilution is believed to cause an increase of the power of the resulting potency. See also *law of infinitesimals*.

Disease Prevention

In conventional medicine, disease prevention is a central part of both patient care and research. *Homeopaths* claim that homeopathy too can prevent people from falling ill. The UK Homeopathic Medical Association, for instance states that:

[…] by boosting the body's own defence system, homeopathy can help heighten resistance to colds, flu and other recurring infections.

Unfortunately, there is no reliable *evidence* to show that this *claim* is true.

Donner Report

Dr. Fritz Donner (1896–1979) was a *homeopath* who was involved in the investigations of homeopathy during the Third Reich. The research programme was by far the largest ever conducted in homeopathy. It covered all levels from *basic* to clinical research. Their results seem to have been spirited away in the hands of the homeopaths. The only *evidence* we have is a detailed report written by Dr. Donner. It suggests that the investigations were supervised by the leading scientists of the era and of high quality. The results were negative on all levels. Donner's full report has now been published and is available on the Internet: http://www.kwakzalverij.nl/699/Der_Donner_Report.

Dosage Forms

Homeopathic preparations can be administered in a range of dosage forms. They include tablets, golbuli, crystals, powders, and liquid preparations (all for oral administration) as well as ointments, creams, lotions, oils, liniments (for topical application), and liquids for intra-venous, intra-muscular, or sub-cutaneous injections. Amongst all these dosage forms, globuli and liquid potencies are by far the most widely used.

Dowsing

Dowsing is a method of problem-solving that uses a motor automatism, amplified through a pendulum, divining rod, or similar device. The best-known from of dowsing is probably water-divining, e.g., finding water wells with the help of a dowsing rod. Dowsing is sometimes used by *homeopaths* as an aid to prescribing and as a tool for identify a *miasm* or toxin load. The only randomized double-blind trial that has tested whether homeopaths were able to distinguish between a homeopathic remedy and *placebo* by dowsing failed to show that it is a valid method.

Drug Picture

Drug picture is the term used by *homeopaths* for the totality of the clinical features caused by the administration of a homeopathic remedy. A drug picture is generated by giving the remedy in question to healthy volunteers in co-called *provings* or *pathogenetic trials*. It includes all the recorded mental, emotional, and physical signs and symptoms displayed or experienced by the volunteers after taking the drug in question. These would then be compiled in the homeopathic *Materia medica* and correspond to the *artificial disease*.

Dynamisation

This term is synonymous with *potentisation* and describes the process whereby the dynamics, *life force*, or *vital force* of a remedy is released or enhanced via *dilution* and *succussion*.

Early Research

Between the years 1820 and 1840, the Prussian medical establishment conducted what was probably the first systematic research programme in homeopathy. Its aim was to test whether a new method resulted in better, faster, or less costly *outcomes*. The *homeopaths* involved hoped that these trials would demonstrate the superiority of their approach. Unfortunately, these hopes were not fulfilled. A century later, a new comprehensive programme of systematic research was imitated in Nazi Germany, and the findings turned out to be similarly negative (see *Donner report*).

Ebola

There are few conditions that *homeopaths* do not *claim* to treat successfully; even the devastating infection Ebola cannot be excluded. The German Zeitschrift fuer Homoeopathie reported as follows at the height of the Ebola outbreak of 2014:

> In mid-October, an international team of 4 doctors travelled to West Africa for three weeks. The mission in a hospital in Ganta, a town with about 40 000 inhabitants on the border of Guinea, ended as planned on 7 November. The exercise was organised by the World Association of Homeopathic Doctors, the Liga Medicorum Homoeopathica Internationalis (LMHI), with support from the German Central Association of Homeopathic Doctors. The aim was to support the local doctors in the care of the population and, if possible, also to help in the fight against the Ebola epidemic. The costs of the three week stay were financed mostly through donations from homeopathic doctors.

Economic Evaluations

Most homeopathic remedies are considerably less costly than conventional medicines. This fact suggests to some people that our health care systems might save money by making more use of homeopathy. However, this assumption ignores crucial factors such as the *cost* for the clinician or the benefit to the patient. The notion that homeopathy can reduce health care expenditure must be tested with rigorous evaluations of the economic impact of using homeopathy. The most authorative *systematic review* of all the 14 studies available to date concluded that it is not possible to draw firm conclusions based on existing economic evaluations of homeopathy.

Effectiveness

The effectiveness of a treatment refers to the clinical effects caused by the therapy (rather than by other phenomena such as the *placebo effect*), as demonstrated under real life conditions. Some proponents of homeopathy have created the term 'real life effectiveness' to describe the effectiveness of the treatment plus all other phenomena that might be involved; however, this is not an accepted concept in conventional medical research.

Efficacy

The efficacy of a treatment is a term that refers to its clinical effects under strictly controlled conditions. It is possible that a treatment is efficacious but not *effective*. For instance, it might have significant adverse effects which overshadow its clinical effects under real life conditions.

Empathy

Empathy is the awareness of the feelings and emotions of other people. It is a key element of 'emotional intelligence', which connects oneself with others, because it is how we as individuals understand what others are *experiencing* as if we were feeling it ourselves. Empathy goes beyond *sympathy*, which might be considered feeling for someone, while empathy might be described as feeling with that person, through the use of imagination. In homeopathy, empathy is important as it is a crucial element of the *homeopathic consultation* and likely to affect the clinical outcome.

Energy

In physics, energy is the capacity to perform work and is measured in units of joules. Energy exists in several forms such as heat, kinetic or mechanical energy, light, potential energy, and electrical energy. In homeopathy and other forms of *alternative medicine*, the term is applied loosely to describe a patient's vitality or the *life force* as postulated by proponents of the long obsolete philosophy of *vitalism*.

Epidemics

Epidemics are outbreaks of disease occurring at the same time in one geographical area and affecting large numbers of people. In homeopathy, epidemics are important because, in its early days, they seemed to provide *evidence* for the notion that homeopathy was *effective*. The results of homeopathic treatment often seemed better than those obtained by conventional means. Today we know that this was not necessarily due to the effects of homeopathy per se, but might have been a false impression caused by *bias* and *confounding*.

Equivalence Study

Most *clinical trials* are *superiority studies* designed to test whether one treatment is more effective than another one. This is fundamentally different in equivalence studies which aim to test whether one treatment is as *effective* as another therapy that has already been fully researched and is generally accepted to be effective for the condition in question. This approach avoids the *ethical problems* that can arise in superiority studies from giving *placebos* to patients who require an effective treatment for their condition. Equivalence studies can have many of the features of superiority studies, but require a different statistical approach and usually need much larger sample sizes.

Ethics

Ethics is the branch of philosophy that involves systematizing, defending, and recommending the moral concepts of right and wrong. Medical ethics is a system of moral principles that apply values and judgments to health care. Its principal values are autonomy, beneficence, and non-maleficence. Some ethicists have argued that, for a range of reasons, the practice of homeopathy might be unethical. For instance, they claim that it necessarily involves deception: patients are not normally told that the principles of homeopathy are biologically implausible and that the best *evidence* fails to show that it is better than *placebo* (if they received this information, they would be unlikely to accept homeopathic treatments). One ethicist therefore concluded that:

> […] homeopathy is ethically unacceptable and ought to be actively rejected by health care professionals.

Evidence

Generally speaking, evidence is the body of facts that leads to a given conclusion. Because the outcomes of treatments such as homeopathy depend on a multitude of factors, the evidence for or against their *effectiveness* is best based not on *experience* but on *clinical trials* and *systematic reviews* of clinical trials. For a more detailed explanation, see Chap. 9 of this book.

Evidence-Based Medicine (EBM)

EBM is defined as the integration of best research *evidence* with clinical expertise and patient values. It thus rests on three pillars: external evidence, ideally from *systematic reviews*, the clinician's *experience*, and the patient's preferences.

Expectation

The prospect of any treatment will almost inevitably generate expectations, both in the patient and in the clinician. Such expectations can significantly influence the clinical *outcome*. Expectations are part of the *placebo* response to medical interventions. They occur inadvertently in most clinical settings. Some characteristics of the *homeopathic consultation* are likely to maximise the expectations of patients. This can contribute to the benefit experienced by patients and is thus a welcome effect in most clinical settings. By contrast, in clinical research, where one usually aims to determine the effect of a therapy per se, expectations would distort the results. In rigorous *clinical trials*, investigators therefore often try to minimise the impact of expectations by 'blinding' patients and/or clinicians to whether the experimental or the control treatment is being administered to any given patient.

Expenditure for Homeopathy

The *cost* of a single homeopathic remedy is usually low. However, on a population basis, the expenditure for homeopathy can nevertheless be substantial. Reliable figures are rare. Americans, for instance, are said to have spent $2.9 billion on homeopathic treatments in 2007, and Germans paid around €500 million on homeopathic remedies in 2013. In 2015, ECHAMP reported that:

> [...] the market for homeopathic and anthroposophic medicinal products in the EU is growing by 6.5% a year. It is now valued at 1.24 billion per year; this represents 7% of the total EU market for non-prescription products.

These figures merely cover the cost of the remedies; if the consultation times and other factors are included, they would increase very substantially. Unfortunately, such data are not currently available.

Experience

Experience is an important topic in homeopathy and deserves detailed consideration. Experience is undoubtedly a most valuable asset. Homeopaths tend to be proud of their collective experience:

- Homeopathy has been around for about 200 years.
- It is popular in many parts of the world.
- Many millions of patients have used it and were satisfied with it.

To assume that this implies homeopathy's *effectiveness* is, however, *fallacious*. Consider, for instance, the case of a *homeopath* whose experience has convinced her that homeopathy is effective. She has studied homeopathy and has 20 years of experience in her clinical practice. She has treated thousands of patients and remembers many who have been cured. Yet her experience might be wrong for a whole host of reasons:

- Clinicians predominantly remember those patients for whom their treatment was successful and tend to forget those where it did not help (recall bias).
- Patients who are not helped by a therapist often do not return; due to this process of self-selection, clinicians can get a distorted picture of their abilities (selection *bias*).
- Some patients employ other treatments without telling their homeopath; if these are effective, the homeopath would get the impression that it was her remedy that did the trick.
- Most homeopaths are *empathetic* and *compassionate* and give plenty of time to their patients; therefore, a *homeopathic consultation* can yield positive effects, even if the homeopathic remedy was nothing more than a *placebo*.

- The prescription of a homeopathic remedy almost inevitably generates a placebo-effect which can produce a positive *outcome* regardless of the effect of the remedy itself.
- Most conditions get better over time and, if this happens, the homeopathic remedy might appear to be effective, while in fact it is not.

All of these phenomena can work in concert in such a way that our homeopath's impression is erroneous.

Next, consider the case of a patient suffering, for example, from an acute respiratory tract infection. He sees a homeopath who, after a long consultation, prescribes a remedy to be taken initially every hour. After a few days, the symptoms are much improved and, after a week, the patient is fully restored. If this type of experience happens several times over, the patient becomes convinced that homeopathy is highly effective. Yet his experience might be wrong for a range of reasons:

- His cold would have disappeared, even if he had not used any treatment at all.
- He might also have taken some painkillers to ease the symptoms, but attributed the relief to the homeopathic remedy.
- As he paid for the homeopathic consultation out of his own pocket, and as he had heard nothing but good things about homeopathy, his *expectations* were high; we know that positive expectations lead to positive outcomes.
- The homeopath took his time, asked questions that conventional clinicians had never asked before, and the patient felt warmly understood. We know that such factors can produce positive outcomes.

Again these phenomena can work together and ease the symptoms a patient is suffering from—even if the homeopathic remedy is entirely *ineffective*.

Experiences of clinicians and patients can be misleading. Experience is not *evidence*, and the plural of anecdote is not evidence but anecdotes.

Faculty of Homeopathy

Founded by Frederick Hervey Foster Quin in 1844 as the British Homeopathic Society, the UK Faculty of Homeopathy is one of the oldest professional organizations for homeopaths. It is the *professional organization* for British homeopaths with a background in medicine, veterinary medicine, dentistry and other statutorily regulated healthcare professions. It provides training pathways in homeopathy in the UK and overseas. British *lay homeopaths* are organized in the Society of Homeopaths.

Fallacy

A fallacy is a popular argument that appears to be logical, but is in fact erroneous. In homeopathy several fallacies are used to support its usefulness or promote its use. For instance, many proponents *claim* that it has stood the test of time suggesting that this proves its *effectiveness*. The argument is fallacious, because the test of time cannot prove effectiveness, as numerous examples from the history of medicine demonstrate. Another classical fallacy is the notion that homeopathy is supported by highly intelligent or famous people and therefore must be good. This argument is fallacious because even highly intelligent or famous people can commit grave errors.

Famous or Notable Quotes on Homeopathy

Homeopathy has always attracted patients from all walks of life. Many people using homeopathy, including numerous celebrities, have commented on their *experience*, so there are many quotes available on the subject. Here is but a small selection of significant quotes from both influential proponents as well as opponents:

Ambrose Bierce

Homeopathist: the humorist of the medical profession.

Roberta Bivins

Homeopathy [...] was instrumental in opening the medical profession to women.

British Government (2010)

The Government takes the view that consumers who chose to use homeopathic medicines should be fully informed about their purpose and assured that standards of quality and safety are maintained. If homeopathic medicines were not subject to any kind of regulatory control, consumers would not have access to such information or insurances.

Anthony Campbell

The great majority, at least, of the improvement that patients experience [after taking a homeopathic remedy] is due to non-specific causes.

Charles Darwin

[Homeopathy] is a subject which makes me more wrath, even than does Clair-voyance: clairvoyance so transcends belief, that one's ordinary faculties are put out of question, but in Homeopathy common sense and common observation come into play, and both these must go to the Dogs, if the infinitesimal doses have any effect whatever. How true is a remark I saw the other day by Quetelet, in respect to evidence of curative processes, viz., that no one knows in disease what is the simple result of nothing being done, as a standard with which to compare Homeopathy and all other such things.

Tom Dolphin

I got into trouble for saying at the juniors' conference that homeopathy is witchcraft. I take that back and apologize to the witches I apparently offended by association.

Ralph Waldo Emerson

Homeopathy is insignificant as an act of healing, but of great value as criticism on the hygeia or medical practice of the time.

Peter Fisher

[Homeopathy] continues to be viewed with great skepticism by many in the medical establishment who cannot comprehend how the very high dilutions used in homeopathic medicine could possibly have any effect.

John Forbes

The favourable practical results obtained by the homeopathists—or to speak more accurately, the wonderful powers possessed by the natural restorative agencies of the living body, demonstrated under their imaginary treatment—have led to several other practical results of value to the practitioners of ordinary medicine.

Joseph W. Freer

It is impossible for a homeopathic physician to be an educated man, or an educated man to be a physician. To say 'homeopathic physician' is as great a solecism as to say 'black white bird'.

Mahatma Gandhi

Homeopathy cures a larger percentage of cases than any other form of treatment and is beyond doubt safer and more economical.

Dizzy Gillespie

There have been two great revelations in my life: The first was bepop, the second was homeopathy.

Ben Goldacre

[…] for the purposes of popular discourse, it is not necessary for homeopaths to prove their case. It is merely necessary for them to create walls of obfuscation, and superficially plausible technical documents that support their case, in order to keep the dream alive in the imaginations of both the media and their defenders.

Peter Hain

My view is that homeopathy and conventional medicines must remain side by side under the NHS to offer the best to patients.

Rudolf Hess

It is known that not just novel therapies but also traditional ones, such as homeopathy, suffer opposition and rejection by some doctors without having ever been subjected to serious tests. The doctor is in charge of medical treatment; he is thus responsible foremost for making sure all knowledge and all methods are employed for the benefit of public health […] I ask the medical profession to consider even previously excluded therapies with an open mind. It is necessary that an unbiased evaluation takes place, not just of the theories but also of the clinical effectiveness of alternative medicine.

Oliver Wendell Holmes

Homeopathy [is] a mingled mass of perverse ingenuity, of tinsel erudition, of imbecile credulity, and of artful misinterpretation, too often mingled in practice […] with heartless and shameless imposition.

Robert T. Mathie

Despite important growth in research activity since 1994, concerns about study quality limit the interpretation of available RCT data. The question whether homeopathic interventions differ from placebo awaits decisive answer.

Yehudi Menuhin

Homeopathy is the safest and more reliable approach to ailments and has withstood the assaults of established medical practice for over 100 years.

James Tyler Kent

While Homeopathy itself is a perfect science, its truth is only partially known. The truth itself relates to the Divine, the knowledge relates to man.

Florence Nightingale

Homeopathy has introduced one essential amelioration in the practice of physic by amateur females; for its rules are excellent, its physicking comparatively harmless—the 'globule' is the one grain of folly which appears to be necessary to make any good thing acceptable. Let then women, if they will give medicine, give homeopathic medicine. It won't do any harm.

Phil Plait

If homeopathy works, then obviously the less you use it, the stronger it gets. So the best way to apply homeopathy is to not use it at all.

Prince Charles

I went to open the new Glasgow Homeopathic Hospital for instance a couple of years ago, I met a whole lot of students who were studying homeopathy, I think, and I've never forgotten when they said to me 'Are you interested in homeopathy' and I thought—I don't know, why do I bother?

Venkatraman Ramakrishnan

They [homeopaths] take arsenic compounds and dilute it to such an extent that just a molecule is left. It will not make any effect on you. Your tap water has more arsenic. No one in chemistry believes in homeopathy. It works because of placebo effect.

Alan Schmukler

When you read about attacks on homeopathy, you have to ask yourself whether you are dealing with pure ignorance, or deceit.

Joe Schwarcz

At the declared homeopathic dose of 200C, the total mass of pills that would have to be consumed to encounter a single molecule of the original substance would be billions of times greater than the mass of the Earth. Yet the label on this product says it contains a 'medicinal ingredient!'

Kevin Smith

A utilitarian analysis […] leads to the conclusion that homeopathy is unacceptable and ought to be actively rejected by healthcare professionals.

Nassim Nicholas Taleb

> Its [homeopathy's] benefits lie in attenuating medical overintervention, acting as a placebo in cases that are marginal, in order to 'distract the patient while nature does the job'.

David Tedinnik

> I also think we can reduce the bill by using a whole range of alternative medicine including herbal medicine, acupuncture, homeopathy [...] We could probably save five per cent of the [NHS] budget.

Armand Trousseau

> To know how to wait is a great science on our part; prudent waiting often explains success; it explains, above all, that obtained sometimes by those of the Hahnemann sect.

Mark Twain

> [I]f another citizen preferred to toy with death, and buy health in small parcels, to bribe death with a sugar pill to stay away, or go to the grave with all the original sweeteners undrenched out of him, then the individual adopted the 'like cures like' system, and called in a homeopath physician as being a pleasant friend of death.

Dan Ullman

> I stand on the shoulders of every homeopathic practitioner and every homeopathic patient before me. And because there have been hundreds of thousands of homeopaths and tens of millions of patients, I am standing tall.

John Weir

> I believe what prevents men from accepting homeopathic principles is ignorance, but ignorance is criminal when human lives are at stake.

Garth Wilkinson

> Hahnemann, without having that end in view, has done more than anyone else perhaps towards the emancipation of woman.

David Wootton

> For the first hundred years or so homeopathy was superior to conventional medicine; it is only for the last hundred years that conventional medicine has had a strong claim to be superior to homeopathy.

Flu and Common Cold

Flu or influenza and common colds are, of course, viral infections. In homeopathy, they are important because they are amongst the diseases most commonly treated with homeopathic remedies. The world's most commercially successful homeopathic remedy, *Oscillococcinum*, is a medication against flu and common cold. Even though there is no good *evidence* that homeopathy is *effective* against the flu, a Harris Poll of

2015 with 2225 US respondents suggested that 19 % of Americans strongly believe that homeopathy is helpful against the flu.

Fluxion

Fluxion is a method of *potentisation* developed by the German homeopath Bernhard Fincke, who patented it in 1869. The potentising effect is not produced as usually by *succussion*, but by the turbulence of the flow of water. Fluxion is used in some mechanical approaches to potentisation.

Freemasonry

Hahnemann became a freemason when he was just 22 years of age. He continued to be attached to freemasonry throughout his life and befriended several distinguished freemasons. At the time, freemasonry harboured ideas of the enlightenment as well as those of the occult, alchemy, cabalism, spiritism, and theosophy. Most biographers of Hahnemann believe that the latter aspects had an important influence on his thinking.

The motto of freemasonry, viz., Aude sapere (Dare to be wise), is taken from Horace. Hahnemann used this motto on the title page of the *Organon*. The influence of freemasonry can also be seen elsewhere: for much of his life, Hahnemann had a preference for the *C30 potency*, but thirty was the degree to which a freemason could be exalted, and it is also the age at which Jesus is said to have commenced his public ministry (Luke 3:23).

Germ Theory of Disease

The germ *theory* of disease holds that many diseases are caused by the actions of specific micro-organisms or germs. The theory was developed and gained gradual acceptance from the mid-1800s. It eventually superseded existing *miasma* or contagion theories of disease. It radically changed the practice of medicine. Today it is long acknowledged as a fact, yet some *homeopaths* seem still to doubt it, for instance, those who adhere to Hahnemann's miasm theory or advise against *immunizations*.

Guiding Symptom

In homeopathy, a guiding symptom is one that provides strong indications for the choice of one specific remedy; such symptoms guide the clinician to the correct remedy, so to speak. 'Guiding Symptoms' was also the title of a homeopathic *Materia Medica* by *Hering* published in 1879.

Hahnemann, Frederick

Frederick Hahnemann was a son of Samuel Hahnemann and his first wife. Frederick initially followed in the footsteps of his father, did a doctorate, became a *homeopath* and even defended his father's *theories* against the attacks from conventional doctors.

Later, he left Germany and travelled and worked in various countries, including Holland, England, and Ireland. Finally, he seems to have moved to America where he is alleged to have made several spectacular cures and eventually vanished. It seems that he suffered from a strange condition that discoloured his skin and rendered him increasingly insane. He left a wife and a son in Germany.

Hahnemann, Christian Friedrich Samuel

Founder of homeopathy, his life and achievements are discussed in the chapters of the first part of this book.

Hahnemann, Melanie

Samuel Hahnemann married his second wife, Melanie, in 1834 when he was 80 years of age and she was around 35 (Melanie never disclosed her exact age). The newly-married couple moved to Paris in 1835, where they established a thriving practice. Initially, Melanie assisted Samuel in writing prescriptions and in recruiting patients; later she began to practice homeopathy even though she had no formal medical training. After Samuel had died in 1843, Melanie continued to practise homeopathy, sometimes assisted by fully qualified physicians. In 1847, she was accused of practising medicine and *pharmacy* without a licence. In her defence, she stated that she held the degree of doctor in homeopathy from the Academy of Pennsylvania. The court nevertheless fined her one hundred francs which she promptly paid. Subsequently, she continued to practise and escaped further prosecution by calling her activities 'medical counselling'.

Hawthorne Effect

The Hawthorne effect refers to the phenomenon that people who are aware of being part of an experiment behave different from normal. Due to the Hawthorne effect, patients being observed after receiving a treatment such as homeopathy can *experience* clinical improvements simply because they are being monitored. The phenomenon is similar to, yet distinct from, the *placebo effect*.

Heilpraktiker

Around the world, homeopathy is currently practiced by two main categories of health care professionals: medically trained *homeopaths* and *lay homeopaths* who, in different countries, come in different guises.

   The German notion of 'Heilpraktiker' (healing practitioner), a non-medically trained alternative practitioner, is best understood by its fascinating history. When the Nazis came to power in 1933, German health care was dominated by lay practitioners who were organised in multiple organisations struggling for recognition. The Nazis reorganised this situation and, at the same time, promoted their concept of *Neue*

Deutsche Heilkunde (New German Medicine) which promoted the integration—perhaps more a shot-gun marriage—of conventional and *alternative medicine*.

The Nazis granted the alternative practitioners official recognition by establishing them under the newly created umbrella of Heilpraktiker. To please the powerful lobby of conventional doctors, they decreed that the Heilpraktiker would be prohibited from educating a second generation of this profession. Thus the Heilpraktiker was destined to become extinct within decades. The Nazi rulers, many of whom were staunch supporters of homeopathy and other forms of alternative medicine, predicted that, by then, alternative medicine would have become an established part of New German Medicine. After the war, the Heilpraktiker went to court to win the right to educate their own students, and today they are a profession that uses homeopathy extensively.

The Heilpraktiker has no mandatory medical training; a simple test to show that he/she knows the legal limits of the profession suffices to practice homeopathy and other alternative therapies.

Heroic Medicine

Heroic medicine is the name for the type of health care that was common in Hahnemann's day. It consisted of treatments that were often detrimental to patients' health, such as blood-letting, purges, toxic drugs, etc. The term is ironic because it was not the physician but the patient who needed to be a hero to survive these tortures. One of Hahnemann's achievements was to contribute to change and progress, by fiercely criticising heroic medicine. See also Chap. 4.

Hess, Rudolf

Hess was the deputy of Adolf Hitler. He was also a strong and powerful advocate of homeopathy. A hospital in Dresden where homeopathy was to be integrated into conventional health care was named after him. Hess was partly responsible for initiating a large-scale investigation into homeopathy (see *Donner report*). After his flight to and arrest in the UK, the hospital was renamed and homeopathy lost its most influential advocate in Germany (Fig. 11.11).

High Potency

A homeopathic remedy that has been *diluted* and *succussed* many times is called a high potency remedy. There is no defined numerical cut-off between high and *low potency* remedies. However, most homeopaths would probably agree that potencies beyond 12C are high potency remedies. According to *Avogadro*, the likelihood of such remedies containing a single molecule of the *mother tincture* approaches zero. Therefore, it seems implausible to assume that high potency remedies can affect human health other than via a *placebo effect*.

Fig. 11.11 Several well known Nazi leaders were keen supporters of homeopathy. In the first row, Himmler and Hess, seen here at the opening of the 12th International Homeopathy Congress at the University of Berlin on 1 August 1937. Photo Scherl/Süddeutsche Zeitung

Holism

Homeopathy is often characterised as being holistic, i.e., concerned not just with the physical side of an illness, but also with its emotional and spiritual dimensions. For instance, *homeopaths* frequently pride themselves in treating the *individual* and not the disease. It would, however, be *fallacious* to assume that homeopathy has a monopoly on whole person care. In fact, holism has always been a core feature of any good type of medicine.

Holmes, Oliver Wendel

Holmes (1809–1894) was an influential US physician and an outspoken *critic* of homeopathy. In 1842, Holmes published Homeopathy and Its Kindred Delusions, in which he advised the following:

> When a physician attempts to convince the person, who has fallen into the Homoeopathic delusion, of the emptiness of its pretensions, he is often answered by a statement of cases in which its practitioners are thought to have effected wonderful cures [...] Such statements made by persons unacquainted with the fluctuations of disease and the fallacies of observation, are to be considered in general as of little or no value in establishing the truth of a medical doctor and all the utility or method of practice.
>
> Those kind friends who suggest a person suffering from a tedious complaint, that he 'had better try Homoeopathy', are apt to enforce their suggestion by adding, that 'at any rate it can do no harm'. This may or may not be true as regards the individual. But it always does very great harm to the community to encourage ignorance, error, or deception in a profession which deals with the life and health of our fellow creatures. Whether or not those who countenance Homoeopathy are guilty of this injustice towards others has to be considered.
>
> To deny that some patients may have been actually benefited through the influence exerted upon their imaginations, would be to refuse to Homoeopathy what all are willing to concede to everyone of those numerous modes of practice known to all intelligent persons by an opprobrious title. So long as the body is affected through the mind, no audacious device, even of the most manifestly dishonest character, can fail of producing occasional good to those who yield it an implicit or even a partial faith. The argument founded on this occasional good would be as applicable in justifying the counterfeiter and giving circulation to his base coin, on the ground that a spurious dollar had often relieved a poor man's necessities.

Homeo-Prophylaxis

See homeopathic *immunisation*.

Homeopath

A person practicing homeopathy is usually called a homeopath. The requirements for carrying this title vary considerably from country to country. Often *lay homeopaths* and *medical homeopaths* exist side by side. In the US, for instance, there are four types of homeopaths:

- Lay homeopaths have no training standards or recognition and are organized in the National Center for Homeopathy.
- Licensed health care professionals, such as medical doctors or *dentists*, have up to 1000 h of training in homeopathy.
- Professional homeopaths are not licensed as health care professionals and have typically around 1000 h of training; their member organization is the North American Society of Homeopaths.
- Registered homeopathic medical assistants have 300 h of training and work under the supervision of a medical doctor.

Homeopathic Children's Hospital, Vienna

The world's first homeopathic childrens' hospital was opened in Vienna in 1879, only 42 years after the Austrian *ban on homeopathy* had been lifted. The hospital was under the management of the order of the Barmherzige Schwestern, and treatment was free of charge, allowing even the poor to be admitted. A single homeopathic physician was responsible for all the patients, most of whom suffered from infectious diseases. Apparently the success rate of the homeopathic treatments was comparable to that of 'allopathic' hospitals. The institution remained in operation until World War I, when it was converted into a military hospital.

Homeopathic Consultation

The initial consultation with a *homeopath* typically lasts for an hour or more. During this time, the homeopath asks questions, listens to the answers, and documents even seemingly insignificant things. As well as noting that the patient is suffering from a runny nose, for instance, a homeopath will look closely at a wide variety of other characteristics of the patient, for example, whether symptoms get worse during the patient's period; whether they are *aggravated* by cold weather or certain foods, etc. In addition, the homeopath might cast an even wider net, noting that the patient prefers the color blue, likes Mozart, hates to be in wide open spaces, needs a lot of sleep, is afraid of heights, dislikes weekends, and so on.

Once the homeopath has established all of these traits, his next task will be to try to find a remedy that fits all of them; in other words, the homeopath must look for a remedy that causes the entire spectrum of characteristics and symptoms reported by his patient. In order to do this, the homeopath relies on *provings* carried out previously which describe the full *drug picture* associated with each homeopathic remedy.

The homeopathic consultation thus differs profoundly from a consultation with a conventional physician. Due to its length and the detailed questioning, patients *experience* more *sympathy*, *empathy*, and *compassion* than from the average mainstream doctor. It is most likely that such phenomena significantly influence the clinical outcome: a recent trial testing this *hypothesis* concluded that:

> [...] homeopathic consultations but not homeopathic remedies are associated with clinically relevant benefits.

Homeopathic Immunisations

Some *homeopaths* advise their patients against immunisations and instead recommend homeopathic immunisations or *homeo-prophylaxis*. This normally entails the oral administration of homeopathic remedies, called *nosodes*. Such remedies are *potentised* remedies based on pathogenic material like bodily fluids or pus.

There is no evidence that homeopathic immunisations are *effective*. After conventional immunisations, patients develop immunity against the infection in question which can be monitored by measuring the immune response to the intervention. No such evidence exists for homeopathic immunisations.

Despite this lack of *evidence*, some homeopaths—particularly those without medical training—continue to recommend homeopathic immunisations. A recent US conference on the topic was advertised with the slogan 'homeo-prophylaxis is a gentle, non-toxic *alternative*'. Such promotion constitutes a serious *risk* for public health: once rates for conventional immunisations fall below a certain threshold, the population would lose its herd immunity, and even those individuals who were immunised will subsequently be at risk of acquiring the infection.

Homeopathics

Homeopathics is the term sometimes used for homeopathic remedies, i.e., preparations manufactured according to a homeopathic *pharmacopeia*.

Homeopathy, Journal of

'Homeopathy', formerly called the British Journal of Homoeopathy, is an international journal published by Elsevier. It is aimed at improving the understanding and clinical practice of homeopathy by publishing articles on clinical and *basic research*, clinical audit, and *evidence*-based practice of homeopathy. Unfortunately, the quality of the articles is often quite poor, and the journal lacks *critical* input. Its impact factor is low, yet it is the leading journal in this field and the only one listed in Medline.

Homosexuality

Therapeutic claims made by *homeopaths* are generally not based on reliable evidence, many are dangerously misleading, and some are even worse. One of the most bizarre *claims* must be that homeopathy can 'cure' homosexuality or erase homosexual tendencies. According to 'abc homeopathy', a popular website in this field, "homosexuality is a perversion caused by the *miasms*". One possible remedy for this 'condition' is pulsatilla, they claim. It goes without saying that none of this has any basis in reality.

Homotoxicology

Homotoxicology is a method inspired by homeopathy which was developed by Hans Heinrich *Reckeweg* (1905–1985). He believed that all or most illness is caused by an overload of toxins in the body. The toxins originate, according to Reckeweg, both from the environment and from the malfunction of physiological processes within the body. His treatment consists mainly in applying homeopathic remedies which usually consist of *combinations* of single remedies, because health cannot be achieved without ridding the body of toxins. The largest manufacturer and promoter of remedies used in homotoxicology is the German firm Heel.

Hormesis

Hormesis is a phenomenon in toxicology that describes how low doses of some stressors have beneficial effects, while high doses cause harmful effects. In toxicology, this is a useful concept; in homeopathy, it amounts to a speculative explanation of the *like cures like* theory. As highly diluted homeopathic preparations no longer contain active molecules, the idea of a beneficial or harmful hormetic response to such remedies seems nonsensical. One expert concluded that:

> Generalizations of the hormesis phenomenon used in support of homeopathy are unfounded.

And another author stressed that:

> Without supporting scientific evidence for the efficacy or purported mechanisms of homeopathy, the term hormesis should not be linked with it in any way.

Hufeland, C.W.

C.W. Hufeland (1762–1832) was a professor of medicine in Jena, Germany, and the editor of one of the most influential medical journals of his time. He was acquainted with *Hahnemann* for more than thirty years. Even though he never fully subscribed to homeopathy, he did support Hahnemann to some degree and, in 1796, published the article in which he first elaborated on the theory of *like cures like* that became the cornerstone of homeopathy.

Hypothesis

A hypothesis is a proposed explanation for a phenomenon. For a hypothesis to be scientific, it ought to be testable. Hypotheses are usually based on observations that cannot be satisfactorily explained with the currently existing scientific *theories*. Even though often used synonymously in common language, in *science*, a hypothesis is not the same as a theory. To mature into a hypothesis, a theory needs supporting *evidence*.

Income of Homeopaths

Homeopathy is practiced in many different countries or settings and with such diversity that the income of practitioners can be expected to vary widely. According to a Salary.com survey of 2012, for instance, the median national annual salary for US family practice doctors is $175 596, for nurse practitioners $90 979, for physician assistants $90 311, and for chiropractors, $131 105. Any of these professionals could practice homeopathy. Actual salaries may vary greatly based on specialization within the field, location of practice, years of experience, and numerous other factors.

Individualisation

In *classical homeopathy*, the choice of the remedy is usually individualised to match the characteristics of each patient. The *drug picture* of the remedy must match the symptoms and signs of the patient as closely as possible. In practice, this means that 10 patients suffering from the same condition, might receive 10 different homeopathic remedies. It is plausible that this individualisation of the treatment is an important factor in enhancing the patient/doctor relationship and maximising the *placebo* response. Thus it can be expected to contribute to the outcome of the treatment, irrespective of the homeopathic remedy administered.

Ineffectiveness

Ineffective treatments are interventions that are no better than *placebo* in producing clinical outcomes. Some proponents of homeopathy are aware of the fact that the *evidence* for homeopathy fails to demonstrate its *effectiveness*, but insist that the data also fail to show its ineffectiveness. An often voiced slogan in this context is 'absence of evidence is not evidence of absence'. This is undoubtedly true but, at the same time, it is fairly irrelevant: in health care, it is wise and *ethical* to use such therapies that are supported by positive proof of effectiveness, and not those for which effectiveness is in doubt. From a scientific standpoint, it is difficult, if not impossible, to prove a negative; therefore, demanding a proof of ineffectiveness seems nonsensical.

Informed Consent

Before starting to treat a patient, all health care professionals, including of course *homeopaths*, have to obtain informed consent. This is not optional but an *ethical* imperative. Informed consent usually includes relevant information about the treatment as well as *alternative* therapeutic options. In the case of homeopathy, it can be argued that the relevant information must include the facts that:

- homeopathy is not biologically plausible,
- its *effectiveness* is unproven,
- not all homeopathic remedies are entirely free of *risks*,
- and better treatments for the condition in question might be available.

Most homeopaths do not obtain such informed consent from their patients. It seems unlikely that patients would consent to being treated, if such information were provided.

Integrative Medicine

Integrative (or integrated) medicine has been defined as a 'comprehensive, primary care system that emphasizes wellness and healing of the whole person'; others have simply characterised it by the slogan 'the best of both worlds'. The aim of integrative medicine is to use *evidence*-based conventional and *alternative* therapies side by side. In the case of homeopathy as part of an integrated approach, there are two main problems: homeopathy is not evidence-based, and homeopathy, according to *Hahnemann*, must not be combined with conventional medicine. Regardless of these facts, most integrative medicine centres do include homeopathy in their therapeutic repertoire.

International Dictionary of Homeopathy

The International Dictionary of Homeopathy is a reference book that emerged from a project sponsored by the European Union. It was prepared in collaboration with the *Faculty of Homeopathy* (FoH) and the Homeopathic Trust UK. Its editor was Jeremy Swayne who was then the dean of the FoH. Many of the leading experts in homeopathy contributed, including the author of this book. The dictionary was intended to facilitate the understanding of homeopathy in its historical context. It was published in 2000 by Churchill Livingston, London.

Isopathy

Isopathy is the use of *potentised* remedies which are derived from the causative agent of the disease that is being treated. It thus does not follow the supreme *law* of homeopathy; instead of *like cures like*, it postulates that identical cures identical. An example of isopathy is the use of potentised grass pollen to treat patients suffering from hay fever. Some of the methodologically best trials that generated a positive result were done using isopathy; they did not therefore test homeopathy and its principal assumption, the like cures like *theory*. They are nevertheless regularly used by proponents of homeopathy to argue that homeopathy is effective.

Jahr, Georg

Georg Jahr (1800–1875) was a friend of *Hahnemann* who converted to homeopathy himself. He became his co-worker in the production of Hahnemann's book Chronic Diseases. Jahr developed the idea that the more peculiar a given symptom is, the higher the most suitable *potency* is likely to be. Jahr remained faithfully at Hahnemann's side for many years, and was even present at the moment of the master's death in Paris.

Jenichen, Julius Caspar

Even in *Hahnemann's* day, homeopathy was taken up by many laypeople who had no medical background whatsoever. Some of these were most colourful individuals, probably none more so than J.C. Jenichen (1787–1849).

Before he became a *homeopath*, he had been a horse-trainer. His physical strength was legendary, and he sometimes displayed it at dinner parties by tearing up silver salvers (a habit which surely diminished his popularity as a dinner guest). Jennichen invented his very own method of *potentisation* which seems to have been based on an idea of Hahnemann's that the master later abandoned: Jenichen believed that the crucial factor for the process of potentisation was not the number of *dilutions* but the number and vigour of the *succussions*. He thus used to shake the vials until 'they rang like a bell'. Ten such shakes, Jenichen decided, were equivalent to one degree of *potency*. He went on to manufacture potencies as high as 60 000 and, for a while, his potencies were highly popular and much sought after.

Kent, James Tyler

Influential US *homeopath* discussed in Chap. 3.

Keynote Symptom

See *guiding symptom*.

Lactose

Milk sugar is used in homeopathy for the production of most solid remedies for oral use. Lactose globuli are sprayed with the liquid *potency* and left to dry. This seems to render the *memory of water* theory even less plausible as an explanation for homeopathy's mode of action. Lactose is also employed as the *diluent* in the *trituration* process, i.e., the *potentisation* of non-soluble materials.

Law of Infinitesimals

This refers to the notion that *potentisation* renders a remedy more potent. It is an axiom of homeopathy, but not a scientific law in the true meaning of the word. See potentisation.

Law of Similars

The is the term often used as the prime axiom in homeopathy claiming that *like cures like*. In the true sense of the meaning, it is not a scientific law. See like cures like.

Lay Homeopath

Lay *homeopath* is the term commonly used for homeopaths who have not studied medicine (some prefer the word 'professional homeopath'). Even during Hahnemann's time, several non-medically qualified individuals took up homeopathy and made important contributions to the field, for instance *Jennichen* or *Boenninghausen*. *Hahnemann* had little choice but to agree with this development, after all, he generally opposed the medicine of his day, which he called 'school medicine' (Schulmedizin), and even his second wife, *Melanie*, became a homeopath without ever having studied medicine. After Hahnemann's death, lay homeopaths began to dominate the field, particularly in the US. Some of them were imprisoned for practising medicine without a licence. Today, some of the most vociferous and influential homeopaths are lay people, for instance, *Schmuckler*, *Ullman*, or *Vithoulkas*.

Legal View of Homeopathy

There have been several legal actions against *manufacturers* of homeopathy (*class actions*) and against homeopaths. An interesting legal assessment of the situation was recently published by an Australian barrister:

> Until such time as homoeopathy can scientifically justify its fundamental tenets [...] it cannot be said that its claims for therapeutic efficacy can be justifiable. This leaves the profession not just exposed to criticisms [...] but potentially open to consumer protection actions directed toward whether its representations are false, misleading and deceptive, to civil litigation when its promises have not been fulfilled, and especially when persons have died, and to criminal actions in respect of the financial advantage that is obtained by its practitioners from their representations.

Life Force

Life force or *vital force* or vital *energy* are the terms used for the metaphysical concept of a power that allegedly animates all organisms. A disturbed life force was, according to *Hahnemann*, the reason why humans fall ill, and he argued that:

> [...] in the state of health, the spirit like vital force (dynamis) animating the material human organization reigns in supreme sovereignty. It maintains the sensations and activities of all the parts of the living organism in a harmony that obliges wonderment.

Similar concepts exist also in other cultures and contexts: chi in China, prana in India, pneuma in ancient Greece, animal magnetism in Messmer's hypnotherapy, the inert in chiropractic, etc. These ideas originate from the concept of vitalism and are now obsolete.

Like Cures Like

Like cures like summarises the principle that *Hahnemann* believed to have discovered while self-medicating with *Cinchona bark*. It subsequently became the first and most important axiom of homeopathy. More details are provided in the first part of this book.

Lincoln, Abraham

In 1854, Abraham Lincoln (1809–1865) was given the task of preparing a state legislative proposal to charter a homeopathic medical college in Chicago. In view of the deep-seated animosity between orthodox medical practitioners and irregular healers, this was not an easy brief. Lincoln and other influential individuals in Illinois lobbied legislators and succeeded in securing the charter. The *Hahnemann* Homeopathic Medical College accepted its first class in 1860, and remained in existence for almost 65 years.

Loschmidt's Number

See *Avogadro's number*.

Low Potency

A homeopathic remedy that has only been *diluted* and *succussed* a few times is called a low potency remedy. There is no defined numerical cut-off between low and *high potency* remedies. Yet most *homeopaths* would call remedies between 1 and 10C low potencies. While it is clear that these dilutions still contain molecules of the *mother tincture*, it is important to point out that, as a rough guide, 1C to about 5C would correspond to the concentration of active ingredients in a cup of tea. Depending on the nature of the *stock*, such a remedy can have active molecules in sufficient amounts to have pharmacological effects or side-effects. By contrast, *potencies* between 5C and 10C are likely to be too weak to have any pharmacological effects. In other words, even for many of the low potency remedies used in homeopathy, pharmacological effects would seem implausible. See also *ultra-molecular dilution*.

Malaria

Malaria is an infection caused by protozoa, usually transmitted via mosquito bites. It became important for homeopathy because it relates to Hahnemann's quinine experiment which made him postulate his *like cures like theory*. Today, many experts assume that *Hahnemann* misinterpreted the results of this *experience*. Yet most *homeopaths* are still convinced that potentised *Cinchona bark* is an *effective prophylaxis* against malaria, and some homeopathic *pharmacies* still offer homeopathic *immunisations* against the infection. In several cases, people who believed themselves to be protected have fallen ill with the infection.

Manufacturers

There are several big and many small firms producing homeopathic remedies; the largest firm in the world is the French firm *Boiron*. Their published gross profit has risen from €291 million in 2012 to €354 million in 2014. Other sizable manufacturers of homeopathics include the Deutsche Homoeopathische Union (Germany), Heel (Germany), and Hylands (US).

Materia Medica

In homeopathy, a materia medica is a collection of descriptions of the totality of the symptoms, signs, emotions, etc., *experienced* by healthy volunteers after ingesting specific homeopathic remedies during *provings*. *Homeopaths* call the totality of these symptoms, signs, etc., *drug pictures*.

Hahnemann was the first to publish such a collection in 1811, and he extended it many times up to the year 1833; he called it Materia Medica Pura. Subsequently, many more such documents were produced. They were often referred to as *repertories*. *Kent's* materia medica became by far the most widely used of them all.

Measles

Many *homeopaths* claim they can treat or prevent childhood infections such as measles. For instance, Steve Scrutton, the director of the UK Alliance of Registered Homeopaths wrote in 2015:

> Many homeopaths feel that it is better for children, who are otherwise healthy, to contract measles naturally. Homeopathy is less concerned with doing this as it has remedies to treat measles, especially if it persists, or becomes severe. Other homeopaths will use the measles *nosode*, Morbillinum, for prevention. Homeopaths have been treating measles for over 200 years with success.

Despite such *claims*, there is no good evidence to show that homeopathy is *effective* for measles or any other infection.

Mechanism of Action

Even enthusiastic *homeopaths* often admit that they fail to understand how homeopathic remedies work. *Hahnemann* believed that his *potentised* remedies unleash the *vital force*, and that this in turn brings about the cure. Such *vitalistic* notions are, however, long obsolete. Several attempts have been made to find explanations which are in line with *science*: secondary structures of water molecules, quantum entanglement, *hormesis*, *nanoparticles*, silicea-hypothesis. However, none of these are accepted outside the field of homeopathy and none would provide a full explanation for the mechanism of action of highly *diluted* homeopathic remedies. A team of authors who recently evaluated all of the current theories *critically* concluded that they are "a collection of terminally flawed trivia".

Medical Homeopath

A medical homeopath is a clinician who has studied conventional medicine and is practising homeopathy. The term is used to differentiate these individuals from lay (or professional) homeopaths who have no formal medical education. *Hahnemann* himself was, of course, a medical homeopath; but even during his lifetime, several prominent *lay homeopaths* emerged, and Hahnemann did not object to them. Later, there were times when, for various reasons, noticeable tensions developed between the two types of homeopaths. Today they seem to coexist relatively harmoniously, even though distinct differences between the two do clearly persist.

Memory of Water

Most homeopathic remedies are *diluted* many times. At each dilution step, the remedy is vigorously shaken, an action called *succussion*. It is claimed to confer some *energy* or information from the less to the higher dilution. Thus a homeopathic remedy is assumed to 'remember' information about the substance it once contained.

Highly diluted homeopathic remedies contain no active molecules and therefore have no pharmacological activity. However, *homeopaths* believe that their remedies work via the *vital energy* or information that has been transmitted to them during dilution and *succussion*, a process which they call *potentisation*. They also believe that, in terms of their health effects, potentisation renders the remedies, not weaker, but stronger.

This assumption, often referred to as the memory of water, is central to homeopathy. Originally, *Hahnemann* had diluted his remedies in order to minimise side-effects; later he claimed to have observed that potentisation renders a remedy more potent. He even warned fellow homeopaths not to carry their remedies in their waist pockets, because the movement might make them too powerful to be used safely.

Today, homeopaths tend to try to explain the memory of water with modern science. For instance, they point to findings about secondary structures of water molecules, or they cite research which implies that, during the process of potentisation, *nanoparticles* are formed which may in turn generate clinical effects. So far, all of these attempts to explain the alleged actions of *ultra-molecular* homeopathic remedies have failed to convince critical scientists.

Miasm

Miasm is a somewhat nebulous concept of disease that *Hahnemann* adopted from the conventional medicine of his day, modified, and made it into a key principle of homeopathy. It describes the acquired or inherited effects of three diseases: the 'itch' (*psora*), gonorrhoea (sycosis), and syphilis. Of the three, psora was considered by Hahnemann to be the most important by far.

Modality

Modality is the term used by homeopaths to describe a condition that makes a person's symptoms better or worse. For example, an abdominal pain might get better when bending over, or worse in rainy weather. The identification of modalities is part of a complete homeopathic history which, in turn, allows the homeopath to select the optimal remedy for each *individual* patient.

Montagnier, Luc

Montagnier (1932–) is a French virologist who won a Nobel Prize in 2008 for the discovery of the HIV virus. Later, he did some research on *ultra-high dilutions* of DNA solutions which some *homeopaths* interpreted as a proof of homeopathy's *law of infinitesimals*. Montagnier was quoted saying:

> I can't say that homeopathy is right in everything. What I can say now is that the high dilutions are right. High dilutions of something are not nothing. They are water structures which mimic the original molecules. We find that with DNA, we cannot work at the extremely high dilutions used in homeopathy; we cannot go further than a 10^{-18} dilution, or we lose the signal.

Many homeopaths nevertheless take this to be an endorsement of homeopathy.

Mother Tincture

A mother tincture, called 'Ur-Tinktur' by *Hahnemann*, is the starting material or *stock* for manufacturing homeopathic *potencies*. Mother tinctures are based on extracts from the source material usually in a water/ethanol mixture. For non-soluble materials, a different process, called *trituration*, is employed. It is often assumed that mother tinctures are all made from plants. This is clearly not the case; they can be based on anything one could possibly think of, for instance, *X-rays* or *Berlin wall*.

Nanoparticles

Nanoparticles are particles that are 1–100 nm in size. According to one currently fashionable *theory*, such microscopic objects are formed during *succussion* of a homeopathic remedy. The theory further postulates that these nanoparticles are responsible for the alleged therapeutic actions of homeopathic remedies. The theory is, however, not accepted by non-homeopaths and does not provide a sufficient explanation for the *mechanism of action* of homeopathy.

Natural History of Disease

The natural history of a disease describes the progress of a medical condition when left untreated. Some diseases, e.g., cancer, tend to get worse as time passes, if left untreated. Many other conditions get better over time, even without any treatment at all. If such conditions are treated with homeopathy, it is easy to confuse the natural history with an effect of homeopathy. The best way to differentiate the two is to conduct a controlled *clinical trial*.

Naturopathy

Naturopathy is a school of medicine which, for therapeutic purposes, employs only the forces and materials which nature supplies. These include plants, heat, cold, water, electricity, diet, etc. Whether or not homeopathy falls under this umbrella is controversial. American naturopaths tend to include it, while most European naturopaths exclude homeopathy. An example for the US position is this recent statement from the American Association of Naturopathic Physicians:

> Homeopathy is taught in the naturopathic colleges and its practice should be included in the naturopathic licensing laws. Naturopathic physicians recognize other licensed practitioners of the healing arts who are properly trained in homeopathy.

In 15 US states, naturopathic board exams include questions on homeopathy.

NHMRC Report

In 2014, the National Health and Medical Research Council of Australia published an influential evaluation of homeopathy which is probably the most thorough and independent ever conducted in the history of homeopathy. It concluded as follows:

> Based on the assessment of the evidence of *effectiveness* of homeopathy, NHMRC concludes that there are no health conditions for which there is reliable evidence that homeopathy is effective. Homeopathy should not be used to treat health conditions that are chronic, serious, or could become serious. People who choose homeopathy may put their health at risk if they reject or delay treatments for which there is good *evidence* for *safety* and effectiveness. People who are considering whether to use homeopathy should first get advice from a registered health practitioner. Those who use homeopathy should tell their health practitioner and should keep taking any prescribed treatments.

National Health Service

From its inception in 1948, the UK NHS has included homeopathy as a therapeutic option free of charge. The 1911 National Insurance Act which insured all British working men already included homeopathy. The integration of homeopathy in the NHS seemed a logical consequence of this situation, yet in 1948, it was controversial amongst homeopaths many of whom felt that it might threaten their independence and identity. Today, only two of the five former homeopathic NHS hospitals survive.

Non-specific Effects

Any therapeutic response has two main components: specific effects and non-specific (or context) effects. The latter describe all phenomena which can determine the clinical *outcome*, but are not due to the treatment per se. The best-known non-specific effect is the *placebo effect*.

Nosode

Homeopathic remedies can be manufactured from all sorts of substances. In the case of nosodes, the *stock* consists of pathological materials, usually from humans. They can include diseased tissue, bodily fluids or discharges, microorganisms, etc. They are turned into *mother tinctures* and subsequently *potentised* into homeopathic remedies.

Nosodes were added to the homeopathic *Materia medica* only in the 1830s and are not in agreement with Hahnemann's *like cures like theory*. Nosodes are promoted and used for homeopathic *immunisations*. A potentised pathogenic substance is administered in the belief that it will prevent the corresponding disease. There is no *evidence*, however, that homeopathic immunisations are *effective*. In 2015, the Canadian Paediatric Society issued the following caution:

> There is scant evidence in the medical literature for either the efficacy or safety of nosodes, which have not been well studied for the prevention of any infectious disease in humans.

Observational Study

An observational study is a non-experimental investigation, usually without a control group. In a typical observational study, patients receiving routine care are monitored as to the treatments administered and the *outcomes* observed.

Such a study design has the advantage of being close to a real-life situation; it is thus relatively easy to recruit large numbers of patients. *Homeopaths* tend to be particularly fond of such studies. However, such investigations have important limitations, which can be demonstrated using what is perhaps the most famous observational study of homeopathy as an example. This was a study of patients attending a hospital outpatient unit for a follow-up appointment. A total of 6544 consecutive follow-up patients were given outcome scores. Of the patients 70.7 % reported positive health changes, with 50.7 % recording their improvement as better or much better. Based on these data, the authors concluded that:

> Homeopathic intervention offered positive health changes to a substantial proportion of a large cohort of patients with a wide range of chronic diseases.

These conclusions are not warranted by the data. Due to the lack of a control group, we cannot be sure whether the observed effects were caused by the homeopathic remedies prescribed, the conventional treatments that many patients had in addition to homeopathy, the *empathetic homeopathic consultations*, a *placebo effect*, a *regression towards the mean*, the *natural history* of the disease, or a mixture of all or some of these phenomena.

Observational studies can unquestionably provide valuable information, but they are not an adequate method for establishing cause and effect between the therapy and the outcome.

Olfactory Route

Hahnemann introduced the olfactory route of administering homeopathic remedies, i.e., inhalation through the nose, in 1827 and occasionally used it throughout his life. After he had moved to Paris, he seems to have employed it more frequently. After Hahnemann's death, however, this method fell into disrepute and experts argued that it was unlikely to deliver sufficient material to the body to generate clinical effects.

Online Consultations

In conventional medicine, online consultations with clinicians are considered to be highly problematic and are therefore discouraged or even prohibited. In homeopathy, this seems to be different; there are numerous websites which offer online consultations with a *homeopath*. One *claims*, for instance, that:

> The online procedure for homeopathic treatment is straightforward, and only requires four simple steps.

Essentially, these involve filling in questionnaires which are allegedly providing the homeopath with sufficient information for identifying the right remedy. It seems obvious that *Hahnemann* would have strongly disapproved of this approach.

Organon

The Organon is *Hahnemann's* major publication, in which he elaborates in detail on the principles of homeopathy and gives fairly definitive instructions for its practice. It is still considered to be the most important text in homeopathy. The title Organon alludes to Aristotle's work on logic, and Francis Bacon's Novum Organon.

Hahnemann kept revising his Organon throughout his life; consequently, it has seen a total of 6 editions. The first edition was published in 1810. Even though completed shortly before Hahnemann's death, the last edition was never published by Hahnemann himself. It fell into the hands of his widow and subsequently her daughter, who married the son of the famous *homeopath* C.M.F. von *Bönninghausen*. From there, it was retrieved after 29 years of negotiations by Haehl and *Boericke* and finally published in 1921.

The text of the Organon is organised in a series of short, numbered paragraphs (in the first edition, there were 271), which are full of repetitions and contradictions and which are not easily accessible for today's readers.

Oscillococcinum

This is perhaps the most commercially successful remedy in the history of homeopathy. In the US alone, it is said to sell US$ 15 million per year. It is marketed by *Boiron*, the world's biggest *manufacturer* of homeopathic products, and has a remarkable history. In the early 1920s, a French physician *claimed* he had discovered the virus responsible for the Spanish *flu*. As it oscillated under his microscope,

Fig. 11.12 Oscillococcinum, a homeopathic preparation supposed to relieve flu symptoms. Manufactured by Boiron

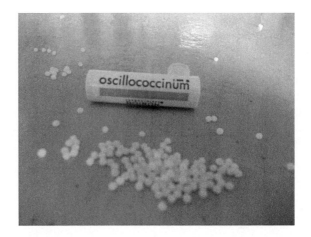

he called it oscillococcus. In the opinion of its discoverer, the virus also caused a whole host of other diseases, including cancer. So far, the existence of this virus has not been independently verified (Fig. 11.12).

Oscillococcinum, is made from the liver and heart of a duck, Anas Barbariae Hepatis et Cordis Extractum. This is because the researcher believed that the virus was present in these organs of the animal. In the actual remedy, the duck organs are so highly *diluted* that no molecule of the duck is present. Oscillococcinum is sold in the C200 *potency* which means that one part of organ extract is diluted at a ratio of 1: 10 000. The dilution is so extreme that it amounts to a single molecule per a multitude of universes.

Given these facts, it seems implausible to assume that the remedy has any effects on human health which go beyond those of a *placebo*. The current *Cochrane* review of Oscillococcinum concludes:

> There is insufficient good evidence to enable robust conclusions to be made about Oscillococcinum in the prevention or treatment of influenza and influenza-like illness. Our findings do not rule out the possibility that Oscillococcinum could have a clinically useful treatment effect but, given the low quality of the eligible studies, the evidence is not compelling. There was no evidence of clinically important harms due to Oscillococcinum.

Outcome Measure

Outcome measure is the term often used for the parameter or endpoint employed in *clinical studies* for quantifying their result or outcome. The optimal outcome measure depends on the nature of the study and might include subjective endpoints such as pain or *quality of life* and/or objective variables such as blood pressure or body weight.

Outcome Study

See *observational study*.

Paradigm

A paradigm is a distinct set of concepts or thought patterns, including *theories*, research methods, postulates, and standards. *Homeopaths* sometimes *claim* that the current paradigm in medicine or science is *biased* against homeopathy and that a paradigm shift is needed to adequately accommodate the concepts of homeopathy. However, a paradigm shift is only necessary in response to critical anomalies and a proposal of a new theory that can encompass older data and also explain the relevant anomalies. Homeopaths have so far failed to make a convincing case for critical anomalies that do not fit the current paradigm, and nor have they made a coherent proposal for a new paradigm.

Pathogenetic Trial

See *provings*.

Peschier, Charles-Gaspard

Charles-Gaspard Peschier (1782–1852) was a leading *homeopath* with influence in French-speaking countries. He dedicated his life to the promotion of homeopathy. Peschier initiated two homeopathic societies and gained influence in the political arena. In 1832, he co-founded the Bibliothèque Homœopathique, the first French homeopathic journal. He was a prolific writer, with a total of 119 papers to his name, 111 of which were on homeopathy.

Pharmacists

Today, most community pharmacists sell homeopathic products in their pharmacies. They are often the only health care professional in contact with a consumer who is about to self-medicate with homeopathic remedies.

In *Hahnemann's* time, the situation was dramatically different. *Homeopaths* would make their own remedies, and many pharmacists felt that homeopaths were thus endangering their livelihoods. This led to fierce disputes between pharmacists and homeopaths. At one stage, the pharmacists of Leipzig even sued Hahnemann and drove him out of town.

Currently, there is growing opposition in the pharmacists' profession to the sale of homeopathic remedies in pharmacies. In 2015, the Chief Scientist of the UK Royal Pharmaceutical Society, for instance, stated:

The public have a right to expect pharmacists and other health professionals to be open and honest about the effectiveness and limitations of treatments. Surely it is now the time for pharmacists to cast homeopathy from the shelves and focus on scientifically based treatments backed by clear clinical *evidence*.

And, in the same year, the President of the Pharmaceutical Society of Australia said that his organisation does not support the sale of homeopathy products in pharmacies:

Our position is that pharmacists must use their professional judgement to prevent the supply of products with evidence of no effect.

Pharmacopeia

A pharmacopeia is a document containing detailed directions for the identification and manufacture of compound medicines. It is usually published by a government or a medical or *pharmaceutical* society. Several countries have their own homeopathic pharmacopeias.

In the US, the Food, Drug, and Cosmetic Act of 1938 focused on *safety*, rather than *efficacy*, and found that those listed in the US Homeopathic Pharmacopeia had met these quality standards. The inclusion in the Act of the Homeopathic Pharmacopoeia appears to have resulted not least from the efforts of Senator Royal Copeland, a *homeopath* and sponsor of the bill.

Placebo

A placebo is an inert treatment, i.e., one that has no effects per se, but can appear to be *effective* through the placebo effect, which essentially relies on *conditioning* and *expectations*. *Hahnemann* frequently used placebos in his clinical practice, for instance, for the purpose of satisfying the wishes of patients who expected to receive a prescription, even though there was no need for any treatment at all. Today placebo administration in routine health care has become all but obsolete and is often considered *unethical*. In research, placebos are used to control for placebo effects in clinical trials which would otherwise render their results unreliable and misleading. They have been used in this way since the early, pioneering trials of homeopathy.

Plausibility

Plausibility relates to the question of whether there are logical explanations for an observed or postulated phenomenon. The plausibility of a therapy hinges on the question of whether its *mechanism of action* is understandable in the light of established facts and *science*. It has been pointed out many times that homeopathy is not plausible. *Homeopaths* tend to counter that science is simply not yet sufficiently advanced to understand how it works. However, this notion is misleading; scientists have pointed out that we do understand that there is no explanation which would be in line with our scientific knowledge as to how homeopathic remedies might work.

Pluralist Homeopathy

Pluralist homeopathy is a variation of Hahnemann's original concepts. It allows or even encourages the use of more than one homeopathic remedy to treat a patient at the same time. The remedies may cover different aspects of the patient's illness. *Hahnemann* was very clear in his instructions that one patient should normally get only a single remedy at any one time (see *unicist* and *purist* homeopathy).

Polychrest

Homeopaths use the term polychrest for a remedy whose *drug picture* encompasses a very wide variety of signs and symptoms as demonstrated through *provings*. Therefore, a polychrest would be employed by homeopaths for an equally wide range of clinical applications.

Post-marketing Surveillance

When a new drug comes on the market, it has been rigorously tested for *efficacy* and *safety* under stringent conditions in test tube experiments, animals, human volunteers, and patients. However, its safety under real life conditions in large populations cannot be entirely certain at this stage. In particular, our knowledge of rare adverse events of a new drug is then still limited. To make sure that rare adverse events do not pose an inordinate risk, the drug must therefore be monitored by post-marketing surveillance. This means that adverse effects must be recorded while it is used by millions of patients. In conventional medicine, this goal is usually achieved by a reporting scheme which notifies the regulator of all observed problems in clinical practice. In homeopathy, no effective post-marketing surveillance systems are in place.

Potency Scales

The production of a homeopathic remedy involves *potentisation* which involves *serial dilution* and *succussion*. Starting with the *mother tincture*, a first *dilution* is made; from it, a second, third, etc., are then manufactured either by hand or by employing specially designed machines.

Dilution can be carried out in different ratios. The *centesimal scale* is commonly used. This is indicated by the letter C. Before or after the letter, there is a number which records the number of serial dilutions performed. Thus the following symbols denote the following dilutions of the mother tincture:

C1 = one dilution 1:100 = 1:100,
C2 = two dilutions 1:100 = 1:10 000,
C4 = three dilutions 1:100 = 1:100 000 000,
C5 = four dilutions 1:100 = 1:10 000 000 000,

and so on.

The most popular potency is C30 which was also frequently used by *Hahnemann*. The dilution of C30 is 1:1 000 000 000 000 000 000 000 000 000 000 000 000 000 000 000 000 000 000 000. This corresponds to not even one molecule of the mother tincture per universe.

Decimal dilutions are popular too. As the name implies, they use steps of 1:10. This is symbolised by the letters D or X. Numerous other potency scales have been used but are less common today; for instance, Hahnemann introduced the LM potency, which is based on a dilution factor of 1:50 000.

Potency

According to homeopathic thinking, potency is the 'power' of a remedy based on the degree to which it has been *potentised*, i.e., *diluted* and *succussed*. *Low potency* remedies are not highly diluted, whereas *high potency* ones are. Low potency remedies contain detectable concentrations of the starting material, whereas high potency remedies contain no detectable amount of the starting material in the finished product. Both types of remedies have been available since the beginning of homeopathy. The full range of homeopathic remedies starts with the undiluted *mother tinctures* and goes to remedies with no measurable concentration.

Potentisation

Potentisation and *dynamisation* are often used as synonyms. They describe the process of manufacturing homeopathic remedies by vigorously shaking (*succussion* and *diluting* them. *Homeopaths claim* that potentisation releases or increases the medicinal power or *potency* of the medicine. In this way, even inert substances such as table salt can become therapeutic, they postulate. In *Hahnemann's* own words:

> In a special process unknown before my time, homeopathy develops the inner spirit-like medicinal powers of crude substances, to a degree hitherto unheard of, and makes all of them exceedingly, even immeasurably penetratingly effective, even those that in their crude state do not have the slightest medicinal effect on the human organism.

Hahnemann, who was not aware of *Avogadro's* work, assumed that matter was infinitely divisible; however much a substance is diluted, he reasoned, there must still be a finite amount there, and that small quantity would suffice to produce an effect. He was wrong of course, but as he lived just before the molecular *theory* was developed, he could not have known. Nevertheless, he commented on the extremely *high potencies* of some of his disciples that "there must be some limit to the thing".

Prince Charles

The British royal family has a long tradition in promoting homeopathy, and Prince Charles is currently the most influential supporter of homeopathy in the UK (Fig. 11.13). For instance, he has lobbied health ministers to promote homeopathy and homeopathic hospitals and he commissioned a report for politicians that

Fig. 11.13 Charles, Prince
of Wales (b. 1948), a well
known advocate of
homeopathy

claimed the *NHS* could save substantial amounts of money if more homeopathy was
used. Yet, whenever he or another member of the royal family are seriously ill, they
seek the help of conventional physicians. Charles' lobbying has repeatedly prompted
sharp criticism; in 2007, an editorial in The Guardian about Charles' attitude towards
homeopathy concluded that:

> Prince Charles must bear in mind that, while meddling by an heir might be deemed improper,
> the same behavior by a king could trigger a crisis.

Professional Organisations

Worldwide there are uncounted professional organizations for *homeopaths*. Important organizations which represent medical homeopaths include the following: Liga
Medicorum Homoeopathica Internationalis (around 10 000 members worldwide),
American Institute of Homeopathy (around 100 registered members), Australia Medical Faculty of Homeopathy (around 200 members), Austrian Association for Homeopathic Medicine (around 800 members), Hellenic Homeopathic Medical Society
(around 100 members), and the UK *Faculty of Homeopathy*.

Provings

The term 'proving' is a mis-translation of *Hahnemann's* term 'Pruefung' which means a 'test'. The English term wrongly implies that some fact is being proven. According to the *International Dictionary of Homeopathy*, provings (also known as homeopathic *pathogenetic* trials or Arzneimittelpruefung, as Hahnemann called them), are defined as the process of determining the medicinal properties of a substance; testing in material dose, *mother tincture*, or *potency*, by administration to healthy volunteers, to elicit effects from which the therapeutic potential, or *Material medica*, of the substance may be derived.

In order to *individualise* their treatment according to the *like cures like* principle, *homeopaths* need to know what symptoms, or *artificial disease*, can be caused by the substances they prescribe. If they treat a patient who suffers from running eyes and nose, for instance, they would be looking for a substance that causes runny eyes and nose in healthy individuals. This is why remedies based on onions might be used to treat conditions like the common cold or hay fever.

But most patients' complaints are usually a lot more complex. For instance, a person might suffer from frequently runny eyes and nose, together with a whole host of other symptoms, many of which might seem trivial or irrelevant to conventional doctors, while for a homeopath, all complaints and patient characteristics are potentially important.

The first proving in the history of homeopathy was Hahnemann's *quinine experiment*, which convinced him that he had discovered that this *malaria* cure causes the symptoms of malaria when taken by a healthy individual. From this *observation*, he deduced that any substance causing symptoms in a healthy person could be used to cure these same symptoms when they occur in a patient.

Provings are normally conducted by administering a mother tincture or a *low potency* to healthy volunteers who subsequently note in minute detail all sensations, symptoms, emotions, and thoughts that occur to them while taking it. These are then carefully registered and eventually form the *drug picture* of that substance.

Of course, throughout the day we all experience all sorts of sensations without apparent reason, whether we have taken a medicine or not. Therefore, simple provings are not reliable and might not describe the specific symptoms caused by the substance in question. Realising this problem, most homeopaths now advocate carrying out provings in a *placebo*-controlled manner, in the hope that this method might generate only symptoms which are specific to the tested substance.

Today, thousands of provings have been carried out; most of them are of very low methodological quality. Their results have been published in reference books called *repertories*. Once they have noted the full range of characteristics of a patient, homeopaths can look up the optimal remedy for each individual case. To ease this process even further, sophisticated computer programs are now available.

Pseudoscience

Pseudoscience is anything that tries to imitate *science*, but neither meets its standards nor abides by its rules. *Critics* have long insisted that much of homeopathy fulfils the criteria for pseudoscience.

Psora

Psora is the most important of the three *miasms* postulated by *Hahnemann* as the causes of all disease. It describes the susceptibility or manifestation of a specific pattern of morbidity which Hahnemann claimed to be caused by the 'itch'. Today, most *homeopaths* attribute less importance to miasms in general and to psora in particular.

Publication Bias

Publication bias is the phenomenon that certain research findings are never published and therefore remain inaccessible to us all. The best-studied aspect is the fact that non-publication happens more frequently with negative than with positive results. The consequence is that, if researchers conduct a *systematic review* of the totality of the research published on one particular topic, they might generate skewed overall findings. It has been argued that, in homeopathy, publication *bias* might contribute to an overall impression that is unrealistically positive.

Purist Homeopath

A purist *homeopath* is a clinician who adheres strictly to the instructions of *Hahnemann*. Since the early days of homeopathy, homeopaths have been divided by this issue: some purists believe that any deviation from Hahnemann's dictum is a travesty that renders homeopathy *ineffective*, while others are convinced that clinicians have an *ethical* responsibility to incorporate new medical knowledge into their practice. An editorial in the British Homeopathic Journal of 1944, for instance, stated that:

> [...] to shut one's eyes to the discoveries of chemotherapy [...] is [...] foolishness. The 'pure' homeopath so-called is a crank living in his own little cell. The complete physician is he who endeavors to know all, and knowing all, to choose what is best for the patient.

Qualitative Research

Research which is not primarily focussed on numerical data but on opinions, impressions, attitudes, views, etc. Such research can never test hypotheses (like 'homeopathic remedies are more than placebos'), but it can nevertheless be used constructively, for instance, to formulate hypotheses: the impression of many patients is that homeopathy is *effective*, therefore the *hypothesis* that it is more than a *placebo* deserves to be tested.

Quality of Life

This term describes the state of well-being of a person. Quality of life can be measured by various means (e.g., validated questionnaires such as the SF36) and can be used to monitor the success of treatments like homeopathy. It can also be employed as an *outcome measure* in *clinical trials* of homeopathy or other therapies.

Quinine Experiment

In 1790, as *Hahnemann* was translating the Treatise on Materia Medica by the Scottish physician Cullen, he came to the passage where Cullen explains the actions of Peruvian or China bark (Cinchona officinalis) which contains quinine, an effective treatment for *malaria*. Hahnemann disagreed with Cullen's explanation that *Cinchona* worked through "a tonic effect on the stomach", and decided to conduct experiments of his own.

Hahnemann ingested repeated doses of Cinchona and noticed that subsequently he developed several of the symptoms characteristic of malaria. This is how Hahnemann later described his experience:

> I took for several days, as an experiment, four drams of good china daily. My feet and finger tips, etc., at first became cold; I became languid and drowsy; my pulse became hard and quick; an intolerable anxiety and trembling (but without rigor); trembling in all limbs; then pulsation in the head, redness in the cheeks, thirst; briefly, all those symptoms which to me are typical of intermittent fever, such as the stupefaction of the senses, a kind of rigidity of all joints, but above all the numb, disagreeable sensation which seems to have its seat in the periosteum over all the bones of the body—all made their appearance. This paroxysm lasted for two or three hours every time, and recurred when I repeated the dose and not otherwise. I discontinued the medicine and I was once more in good health.

He concluded that he had discovered something of great general importance: there seemed to be a similarity between the symptoms of a disease and the symptoms caused by a drug that is *effective* in treating that disease. After several more experiments, Hahnemann became convinced that he had, in fact, discovered a *law* of nature: similia similibus currentur (*like cures like*), which became the basis of homeopathy. In 1796, he published his theory in an article entitled Essay on a New Principle. In 1806, he wrote a more detailed treatise which he called The Medicine of Experience and, in 1810, the first edition of his major work the *Organon* followed.

Since then, several attempts have been made to reproduce Hahnemann's quinine experiment. The results of the most rigorous of these replications have failed to confirm Hahnemann's original findings: neither Cinchona bark nor its main ingredient, 'ine, produce the symptoms of malaria in a healthy person.

The dose Hahnemann took contained about 400–500 mg of quinine. After ingesting it, he felt languid and drowsy (hypotension); he noticed palpitations (ventricular tachycardia), pulsation in the head (headache), redness in cheeks (rash), prostration through limbs (general weakness), thirst (fever), and cold fingers and feet with trembling, which are indicative of an allergic reaction. The most likely cause of the symptoms experienced by Hahnemann is, according to many experts today, an allergic reaction to 'ine. It would follow that Hahnemann described his symptoms accurately, yet he was mistaken in his interpretation of the event. If this assumption is correct, the principle axiom of homeopathy is based on a misunderstanding.

Reckeweg, Hans Heinrich

Dr. Reckeweg was a German homeopathic physician who practised *complex homeopathy* and developed *homotoxicology* as well as homaccorde, i.e., the administration of multiple *potencies* of the same remedies in a single preparation. He started a commercially successful line of *combination remedies*. The remedies are recommended for conventional diagnostic indications, but treated with homeopathically manufactured mixtures. According to proponents, they therefore built a bridge between conventional and homeopathic medicine. In the early 1970s, Reckeweg sold 50 % of his company to the Delton Group and moved to the US.

Regression Towards the Mean

Regression towards the mean is the phenomenon describing the fact that, over time, extreme values tend to move towards less extreme values. Patients normally consult clinicians when they are in somewhat extreme situations (e.g., when they have much pain). Because of the regression towards the mean, they are likely to feel better the next time they see their clinician. This change is regardless of the effects of any treatment they may have had. Thus regression towards the mean is one of several phenomena that can make an *ineffective* therapy appear to be *effective*.

Regulation

In healthcare, regulations are agreements enforceable by law to protect the public, consumers, and patients. In homeopathy, we have to consider the regulation of homeopathic products as well as that of homeopathic practitioners. Both sets of regulations vary considerably from country to country, but generally speaking, they are less rigorous than those for conventional drugs and practitioners. In 2010, the British government issued a statement saying that:

> [...] if regulation was applied to homeopathic medicines as understood in the context of conventional pharmaceutical medicines, these products would have to be withdrawn from the market as medicines.

In America, the regulation of homeopathy is currently being reconsidered. The US Food and Drug Administration (FDA) filed a request in 2015 for comments from the public about homeopathics to determine whether its limited regulatory oversight of these products was "appropriate to protect and promote public health". The FDA then held a public hearing featuring *homeopaths* and representatives of the homeopathic industry, as well as drug *safety* experts. In the same year, the Federal Trade Commission organized a public workshop on the advertising of homeopathics to determine whether it might violate US regulations, which prohibit deceptive acts or practices affecting commerce.

Repertory

A repertory is an index of the homeopathic *Materia medica* ordered by symptom. A list of remedies is provided for each symptom. Most modern day repertories use *Kent's* Repertory as their basis. Many electronic repertories are available to facilitate the task of identifying the optimally matched remedy (*similium*).

Research Activity in Homeopathy

Compared to other fields of health care, the research activity has always been modest. Up to the mid-1990s, only 100 or less articles per year were listed in Medline, the largest database for medical publications. In 2005, a peak was reached with 233 articles, but thereafter the annual output declined. To put these numbers in perspective, on the topic of two single classes of conventional drugs, for instance, beta blockers and statins, we find consistently more than 2000 Medline-listed articles per year.

The reasons for this relatively low level of research activity might be complex. *Homeopaths* tend to claim few research funds are available in their field. However, it could also be argued that most homeopaths have little interest in research, which would also explain why the field is unable to generate more research funds.

Risk–Benefit Analysis

Many proponents argue that homeopathy is *safe* and therefore valuable. This notion ignores the fact that the value of any therapy is not determined by its *risks* (nor by its *effectiveness*) alone, but by the balance between its risks and its benefits. If a treatment has no benefits or effectiveness, its risk–benefit balance is unlikely to be positive.

Risks of Homeopathy

See *safety*.

Royal London Homeopathic Hospital

The Royal London Homeopathic Hospital, recently renamed as the Royal London Hospital for Integrated Medicine, has a long history and is perhaps the most influential homeopathic hospital in the world (Fig. 11.14). It was founded in 1849 by Dr. Frederick Hervey Foster Quin. In 1895, a new and larger hospital was opened on its present site in Great Ormond Street. Many famous homeopaths have worked there, including Robert Ellis Dudgeon, John Henry Clarke, James Compton Burnett, Edward *Bach*, Charles E. Wheeler, James Kenyon, Margaret Tyler, Douglas Borland, Sir John Weir, Donald Foubister, Margery *Blackie*, and Ralph Twentyman.

In 1920, the hospital received Royal Patronage from the Duke of York, later King George VI, who also became its president in 1924, and in 1936, the hospital was

Fig. 11.14 Royal London
Homeopathic Hospital, now
known as the Royal London
Hospital for Integrated
Medicine

honoured by the Patronage of His Majesty the King, gaining its Royal prefix in
1947. Today, Queen Elizabeth II is the hospital's patron.

On 18 June 1972, 16 of the hospital's doctors and colleagues on the board were
killed in a plane crash. During the following years, several reductions in size and
income took place. From 2002 to 2005, the hospital underwent a £20 million rede-
velopment and, in 2010, its name was changed to the Royal London Hospital for
Integrated Medicine.

Royal Pharmaceutical Society (UK)

During the 200 years of homeopathy's existence, *pharmacists* have had an ambiva-
lent relationship with it. At first, they opposed it and even sued *Hahnemann*. Later,
many pharmacists became much more tolerant and most community pharmacists
sold homeopathic remedies. More recently, some pharmacists have reasoned that
the *evidence* for homeopathy is negative and that pharmacists should therefore stop
supporting it. The following statement by the UK Royal Pharmaceutical Society of
2015 is an example of this development:

- There is no evidence to support the clinical efficacy of homeopathic products beyond a
  placebo effect, and no *scientific* basis for homeopathy.

- Pharmacists selling homeopathic products must be competent to do so and be able to discuss with patients the lack of evidence for the *efficacy* of homeopathic products and their formulation.
- Pharmacists should ensure, wherever possible, that patients do not stop taking their prescribed conventional medication when they take a homeopathic product.
- Pharmacists should be aware that patients requesting homeopathic products may have serious underlying undiagnosed medical conditions that would require referral to another healthcare professional.
- Pharmacists should not knowingly sell homeopathic products for serious medical conditions. However, it is recognised people will self-select homeopathic products from open display often without consulting a pharmacist.
- Royal Pharmaceutical Society does not endorse homeopathy as a form of treatment.

Safety

Homeopathy is generally considered to be a safe therapy. In fact, it could be seen as one of *Hahnemann's* achievements that he recognised the dangers of the *heroic medicine* of his day and came up with an *alternative* that had far fewer side-effects. Yet it is not true that homeopathy is entirely *risk*-free.

How can homeopathy cause harm? There are several possibilities:

- Not all homeopathic remedies are *highly diluted*. A *mother tincture* or *low potency* of arsenic are strictly speaking homeopathic remedies, yet unquestionably lethal.
- *Quality control* of the manufacturing processes might not be sufficiently robust, and this could result in remedies containing harmful substances in sufficiently large amounts to cause harm.
- Homeopathy might replace conventional therapy for a serious condition. For instance, a cancer patient might use homeopathy to cure his condition, a decision which could cost his life. Most *homeopaths* would not recommend this course of action, but there are a plethora of *claims* on the Internet suggesting that homeopathy can cure all sorts of life-threatening conditions. And, of course, Hahnemann himself was adamant that homeopathy was the best medicine for any condition and must never be combined with conventional treatments.

Schüssler, Wilhelm

The German Physician Wilhelm Schüssler (1821–1898) developed a derivative of homeopathy called Biochemie, based on physiological considerations by Jakob Moleschott (1822–1893) and Justus von Liebig (1803–1873). Schüssler started out as a *homoeopath*, but soon began to experiment with his mineral salt preparations called Schüssler salts. His work was continued by Dietrich Schöpwinkel (1876–1946), who added new preparations to the system. Schüssler salts have in common with homeopathics that they are *highly diluted*, and therefore devoid of active ingredients and pharmacological effects.

Science

Science can be defined as the identification, description, observation, experimental investigation, and theoretical explanation of phenomena. See also *pseudoscience*.

Scientability

Scientability is a term coined by the German Journalist C. Weymayr, suggesting that some subjects, e.g., homeopathy, entirely lack *plausibility* and thus do not merit *scientific* investigation. In Weymayr's own words:

> Homeopathy has even managed to present itself as scientifically justified by using evidence-based medicine. With the aim of highlighting the speculative character of homeopathy and other procedures and of preventing evidence-based medicine from getting damaged, the concept of scientability is introduced […] This concept only approves of clinical studies if the intervention that is to be tested does not contradict definite scientific findings.

Scientific Law

A scientific law or law of nature is an analytic statement of invariable facts of the physical world; it can be subject to change in the light of further *evidence*. The 'laws' of homeopathy, i.e., the *law of similars* and the *law of infinitesimals*, do not fulfill these criteria and are thus not scientific laws but, at best, *theories*.

Self-healing

Self-healing is the natural capacity of our body to repair and heal itself. In homeopathy, this is an important concept: according to *Hahnemann* and his followers, homeopathic remedies are *effective* due to their ability to stimulate the self-healing capacity of the body. Even though this may sound *plausible* to *homeopaths*, there is no *scientific evidence* to demonstrate that this assumption is true.

Serial Dilution

Serial dilution is the process used in the *manufacture* of homeopathic remedies. It is a sequence of separate *dilutions* of the same *stock*, where each dilution is done at the same proportion depending on the *potency* scale chosen. Each dilution step is followed by *succussion* to yield the next higher potency of the remedy.

Seven Things to Remember Before Consulting a Homeopath

Before patients put their health into the hands of a *homeopath*, it might be worth remembering seven simple points:

1. Homeopathy was invented by Samuel *Hahnemann* about 200 years ago. At the time, our understanding of the *laws* of nature was incomplete, and Hahnemann's ideas seemed less implausible than today.

2. Many consumers confuse homeopathy with *herbal* medicine; yet the two are fundamentally different. Herbal medicines are plant extracts with potentially active ingredients. Homeopathic remedies may be based on plants (or anything else you can think of), but are typically so dilute that they contain not a single molecule from the plant.
3. Homeopaths claim that their remedies do not work pharmacologically, but via some *energy* or *vital force*. They are convinced that the process of preparing the homeopathic *dilutions* transfers some *vital energy* from one to the next dilution, and cite all sorts of theories to explain how this 'energy transfer' might work. None of these assumptions has ever been accepted by mainstream *scientists*.
4. Homeopathic remedies are usually prescribed according to the *like cures like* principle; but there are other forms of homeopathy, too. For instance, *clinical homeopathy* does not follow the like cures like principle.
5. The *clinical trials* of homeopathy are broadly in agreement with these insights from *basic science*. Today, more than 300 such studies have been published; if we assess the totality of this *evidence*, we have to conclude that it fails to show that highly diluted homeopathic remedies are anything other than *placebos*.
6. Nevertheless, many patients do get better after taking homeopathic remedies. The best evidence available today clearly shows, however, that this improvement is unrelated to the homeopathic remedy per se. It is the result of an *empathetic*, *compassionate* encounter with a homeopath, a placebo response, or other factors which experts often call 'context effects'.
7. The widespread notion that homeopathy is completely free of risks is misleading. The highly dilute remedy itself might be harmless, but this does not necessarily apply to the homeopath. Whenever homeopaths advise their patients to forgo *effective* conventional treatments for a serious condition, they endanger lives.

Significance

Statistical significance describes the likelihood with which a given research result is due to chance. Often it is expressed by providing a so-called p-value, i.e., a probability. The commonly used p-value of 0.05 indicating statistical significance means that the chances are 5 in 100 that the result in question is due to chance.

Clinical significance or relevance are terms often used to describe the likelihood that a clinical result is important in a clinical context. For instance, a study might show that a homeopathic treatment has lowered systolic blood pressure by 3 mmHg; this could well be statistically significant, but few experts would call it clinically significant.

Similimum

Similimum is the term *homeopaths* use for a remedy that is optimally matched to the individual signs and symptoms of a patient. Homeopaths identify the similimum through an often lengthy consultation, using a *repertory* to match the *drug picture*

with the symptoms. The similimum is the remedy which is considered the most likely
to bring about a cure.

Social Desirability

Social desirability describes the phenomenon that humans tend to respond in accor-
dance to social norms and in the manner which they believe is expected from them.
Social desirability can be a powerful *confounding* variable in *clinical trials*, as well
as in clinical practice. For instance, a patient might tell his *homeopath* that the prescribed remedy was *effective*, not because of the way he feels, but because he wants
to return the kindness he has received from the homeopath. In turn, the homeopath
would get the erroneous impression that his remedy had been effective.

Source Material

Source material or *stock* is the substance from which a given homeopathic remedy
has been produced and from which its therapeutic properties are thought to originate.
Source materials are named on the packaging of the remedy; they are often botanical
by nature, but can also be minerals, synthetic chemicals, pathogens, human or animal
tissues or materials, and even immaterial items such as *X-rays*.

Specific

In therapeutics, specific effects are those effects of a medicine that are directly caused
by the medicine (or its metabolites) and not by other phenomena such as the *placebo
effect* or the *natural history* of the disease.

  In homeopathy, the specific refers to the homeopathic remedy specifically indicated for a particular condition or disease. For instance, *Arnica* is a popular specific
for cuts and bruises.

Stapf, Johann Ernst

Stapf (1788–1860) was a friend and supporter of *Hahnemann* who is said to have
been the very first physician to adopt homeopathy in his clinical practice. Stapf was
one of Hahnemann's most enthusiastic volunteers for conducting multiple *provings*.
Later he became a famous clinician in his own right. In 1835, he was called to treat
Queen Adelaide of England.

Steiner, Rudolf

See *anthroposophic medicine*.

Stock

See *source material*.

Succussion

After *dilution*, a homeopathic remedy is shaken vigorously to generate the next higher *potency*. *Homeopaths* call this process succussion ('succutere' is the Latin verb for 'to shake'). The method of succussion is not standardised and varies between manufacturers. *Hahnemann* allegedly used his Bible as a pad for succussion and initially advised ten downwards strokes, but later only two 'least the remedy be made too potent'. Other methods of *potentisation* are *fluxion* and *trituration*.

Superiority Trials

Superiority trials are *clinical studies* where the *effectiveness* of typically two treatments is compared in order to determine which one is better than the other. *Placebo* controlled trials, for instance, are superiority trials testing whether the experimental treatment is superior to placebo. The statistical analysis of superiority trials differs from that of *equivalence studies*, and the former usually require smaller sample sizes than the latter.

Swedenborg, Emanuel

Swedenborg (1688–1772) was an inventor, theologian, and mystic who had a strong influence on the thinking of prominent homeopaths, particularly *Kent* (Fig. 11.15). Swedenborg believed that every material phenomenon has a spiritual counterpart. Consequently, *homeopaths* influenced by him stress the spiritual dimension of illness and treatment. A protestant sect was founded in Swedenborg's name in 1788.

Swiss Government Report

This name is often given by *homeopaths* to a report allegedly commissioned by the Swiss government evaluating the *effectiveness* of homeopathy. The report which arrived at generally positive conclusions was, however, not actually conducted, commissioned, or funded by any government. On the contrary, it was generated by known proponents of homeopathy and, more importantly, *critical* analysis discloses it as deeply flawed and unreliable.

Sympathy

Sympathy describes the feeling of caring about or being sorry about someone else's problems, or the ability to feel for someone else. Even though the two terms are often used as synonyms, sympathy is not the same as *empathy*. Homeopaths are often able to show sympathy during a lengthy *homeopathic consultation*, and it is likely that this phenomenon affects the clinical *outcome* and significantly contributes to the popularity of homeopathy.

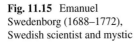

Fig. 11.15 Emanuel
Swedenborg (1688–1772),
Swedish scientist and mystic

Systematic Reviews and Meta-analyses

In most areas of health care, there is an abundance of *clinical trials*, the results
of which are usually not entirely uniform: some suggest that a given treatment is
effective, while others suggest the opposite. Homeopathy is no exception; well over
300 clinical trials of homeopathy are currently available, and predictably some are
positive, while others are negative.

In this situation, it is tempting to *cherry-pick*, i.e., to choose those studies which
confirm one's prior belief as *evidence* to convince others. Obviously, this approach is
misleading and counter-productive. What is needed is a method that avoids cherry-
picking and generates conclusions which are reliable. This is precisely what systematic reviews aim to achieve.

A systematic review is a project where the totality of the available evidence related
to a well-defined research question is summarised and *critically* analysed in order
to provide the most reliable answer possible. Systematic reviews are thus valuable
in guiding evidence-based therapeutic decisions. They minimize the *bias* inherent in
each individual study and save others from having to do the hard work of analysing
the often substantial numbers of clinical trials in order to find the answer to the
relevant clinical question.

If a systematic review employs a mathematical approach for pooling the data of various clinical trials to generate a new quantitative overall result, we call it a meta-analysis.

Tessier, Jean-Paul

Tessier (1811–1862) was one of the first prominent *homeopaths* in France. He became famous, not least for some early research into the *effectiveness* of homeopathy. His *epidemiological* studies compared homeopathic with conventional treatments in large populations and seemed to show that homeopathy yielded superior outcomes.

Theory

A theory is the result of abstract thinking, for example, regarding generalized explanations of how nature works. A theory provides an explanatory framework for a set of observations. From the assumptions of the explanation there follow a number of possible *hypotheses* that can be tested in order to provide *evidence* for or against the theory.

Therapeutic Claims

Therapeutic *claims* are statements of therapeutic *effectiveness* for specific diseases or conditions, e.g., therapy x is effective in treating disease y. Because homeopathy aims, not to treat specific conditions, but to cure sets of symptoms—*homeopaths* often pride themselves in not treating diseases, but patients—homeopaths believe they are, in fact, able to treat most if not all conditions. It is thus possible to find therapeutic claims suggesting that homeopathy is useful for almost any human condition. Popular therapeutic claims include the idea that homeopathy is effective for *flu*, the common cold, and allergies; less common claims are that it cures cancer and even *homosexuality*.

Therapeutic Relationship

The term describes the relationship between a patient and his or her clinician. In homeopathy, therapeutic relationships tend to be particularly intense, not least due to the length of time a *homeopathic consultation* usually takes. There is *evidence* to suggest that, in homeopathy, the therapeutic relationship is a determining factor in the clinical *outcome*.

Trituration

Trituration is the method used for manufacturing *potencies* of insoluble solid *stock*. It consists in grinding the source material in another solid material, usually lactose. To produce liquid potencies from this, the trituration is then dissolved in water to continue the *potentisation* by *succussion* as with a normal liquid potency.

Ullman, Dana

Ullman (1951–) is a US *homeopath* and journalist, and a particularly outspoken entrepreneur and promoter of homeopathy, who has written several books on the subject and campaigns tirelessly for wider acceptance of homeopathy. He sees himself as the "spokesperson for US homeopathic medicine'. More *critical* thinkers, however, struggle to take Ullman seriously, and even a judge once gave this verdict of him:

> Gregory Dana Ullman […] outlined the theory of homeopathic treatment and presented his opinion as to the value and effectiveness of homeopathic remedies. The Court found Mr. Ullman's testimony to be not credible. Mr. Ullman's bias in favour of homeopathy and against conventional medicine was readily apparent from his testimony. He admitted that he was not an impartial expert but rather is a passionate advocate of homeopathy. He posted on Twitter that he views conventional medicine as witchcraft. He opined that conventional medical science cannot be trusted […] Mr. Ullman's testimony was unhelpful […] his opinions regarding its [homeopathy's] *effectiveness* was unsupported and *biased*. The Court gave no weight to his testimony.

Ultra-Molecular Dilutions

This term is often used for homeopathic *potencies* that are too dilute to contain a single molecule from the *mother tincture*. This is normally the case for all potencies higher than C12 or D24. See also *Avogadro's* number, *low potency*, and *high potency*.

Unicist Homeopathy

School of homeopathy that insists on following Hahnemann's dictum of using only a single remedy for one patient at any one time. See also *pluralist homeopathy*.

Vaccination

Edward Jenner (1749–1823) made his discovery of smallpox vaccination during the lifetime of *Hahnemann*, who was impressed with this medical breakthrough (Fig. 11.16). He commented that:

> The widespread use of vaccination has so effectively put an end to all *epidemics* of the terribly deadly smallpox that the present generation no longer has any clear idea of this hideous bygone scourge.

Despite the monumental success of this and many other forms of *immunisation*, and despite the fact that some proponents of homeopathy *claim* that homeopathy works via the same principles as immunisations, many *homeopaths* soon became highly sceptical about immunisations. Today there is evidence that homeopaths from across the world tend to advise their patients against vaccinations.

There seem to be several reasons for this stance:

• Some homeopaths believed to discover that immunisations can cause chronic diseases which are often difficult to cure.

Fig. 11.16 Edward Jenner (1749–1823). Memorial in Gloucester cathedral. Public domain, https://commons. wikimedia.org/w/index.php? curid=30446420

- Some dispute the evidence showing that immunisations are the main reason for controlling major infectious diseases.
- Some believe that *homeopathic immunisations*, i.e., the use of *nosodes* for the *prevention* of infections, are *effective* and free of side-effects.

Vega-Test

The vega-test (also sometimes called 'electro-dermal test') is a method by which, according to its proponents, it is possible to measure the body's electrical *energy* with an instrument that uses an electrical circuit passing through the patient. Some *homeopaths* use it to determine the optimal homeopathic remedy for their patients. *Scientific* tests have shown no validity for the vega-test, yet it is still in widespread use.

Veterinary Homeopathy

After *Hahnemann* gave a lecture on the subject in the mid-1810s, homeopathy was used for treating animals. Von *Bönnighausen* was one of the first influential proponents of veterinary homeopathy. However, veterinary medical schools tended to reject homeopathy, and the number of veterinary *homeopaths* remained small. In the 1920s, veterinary homeopathy was revived in Germany. Members of the Studiengemeinschaft für tierärztliche Homöopathie (Study Group for Veterinary Homoeopathy), which was founded in 1936, started to investigate this approach systematically.

Today, veterinary homeopathy is popular, not least because of the general boom in *alternative medicine*. *Prince Charles* has become a prominent advocate, who claims to treat his own livestock with homeopathy. In many countries, veterinary homeopaths have their own *professional organisations*. In other countries, however, veterinarians are *banned* from practising homeopathy. In the UK, only veterinarians are allowed to use homeopathy on animals (while anyone, regardless of background, can use it on human patients). In the US, homeopathic vets belong to the Academy of Veterinary Homeopathy.

Vienna School of Medicine

The First Vienna School of Medicine was founded in 1365 by Gerard van Swieten (1700–1772), a pupil of Herman Boerhaave (1668–1738). Its aim was to put medicine on *scientific* foundations by using unprejudiced clinical *observation*, botanical and chemical research, and the introduction of simple but powerful remedies. Anton Störck (1731–1803), a follower of these concepts and director of Austrian public health and medical education in Vienna, was the first scientist to systematically test the effects of poisonous plants such as hemlock, henbane, and meadow saffron. *Hahnemann* studied under Störck's pupil, Joseph Quarin, during his time in Vienna and was clearly influenced by Störck's ideas. Hahnemann's method of testing his remedies on healthy individuals in *provings* is said to have originated from the ideas he learned about in Vienna.

Vis Medicatrix Naturæ

This is the Latin expression for the healing power of nature. Like most other *alternative* practitioners, *homeopaths* attribute great importance to it and believe it to be mediated by the *vital force*. *Hahnemann* wrote in his *Organon* that:

> In the state of health, the spirit-like vital force (dynamis) animating the material human organization reigns in supreme sovereignty. It maintains the sensations and activities of all the parts of the living organism in a harmony that obliges wonderment.

Vital Force

See *life force*.

Vitalism

Vitalism is the now obsolete metaphysical concept that life depends on a *vital force* distinct from chemical, physical, or other principles. It is a concept found in many different cultures and healing traditions, e.g., chi in China, pneuma in ancient Greece, and prana in India. The common denominator is the assumption that a metaphysical *energy* animates all living systems.

Hahnemann believed that homeopathic remedies act through a vital force released during the process of *potentisation*. The issue of the vital force soon divided the realm of homeopathy into those who advocated *ultra-high potencies* and those who felt such remedies were the stuff of fantasy, between those who believed every word Hahnemann wrote and those who felt that homeopathy must evolve with new knowledge and *science*.

Vithoulkas, George

George Vithoulkas (1932–) is a Greek teacher of homeopathy, a strict follower of *Hahnemanns* doctrines, as well as one of the most influential *homeopaths* of the present age. He is a *lay homeopath* who studied homeopathy in South Africa and received a diploma in homeopathy from the Indian Institute of Homeopathy in 1966. He then returned to his native Greece, where he currently practises and teaches *classical homeopathy*. Vithoulkas has written many books and received several awards and honorary titles, but he has published as good as no research whatsoever into homeopathy or any other field.

X-Potency

Same as *decimal potency*, based on 1:10 or decimal *dilutions*.

X-Ray

The X-ray remedy is an example of a homeopathic preparation that is not based on any material *stock* at all. Similar remedies are luna (moonlight) or sol (sunlight). The *mother tincture* of the X-ray remedy consists of pure *diluent* that has been exposed to X-rays. It can then be *potentised* just like any other *source material*. According to the *like cures like theory*, it is used to treat inflammations of the skin (X-ray exposure can, of course, cause skin irritation.). There is, however, no good *evidence* that the X-ray remedy has any effects beyond *placebo*.

References and Further Reading

Altunç, U., Pittler, M.H., Ernst, E.: Homeopathy for childhood and adolescence ailments: systematic review of randomized clinical trials. Mayo Clin. Proc. **82**(1), 69–75 (2007)

Avina, R.L., Schneiderman, L.J.: Why patients choose homeopathy. West. J. Med. **128**(4), 366–369 (1978)

Baum, M., Ernst, E.: Should we maintain an open mind about homeopathy. Am. J. Med. **122**(11), 973–974 (2009). doi:10.1016/j.amjmed.2009.03.038

Bellavite, P., Signorini, A.: Homeopathy: A Frontier in Medical Science: Experimental Studies and Theoretical Foundations by Paolo Bellavite. North Atlantic Books, Berkeley (1995)

Bivins, R.: Alternative Medicine?: A History. OUP, Oxford (2010)

Bornhöft, G., Matthiessen, P.: Homeopathy in Healthcare: Effectiveness, Appropriateness, Safety, Costs. Translated by Saar, M.M. Springer, Berlin (2011)

Brien, S., Lachance, L., Prescott, P., McDermott, C., Lewith, G.: Homeopathy has clinical benefits in rheumatoid arthritis patients that are attributable to the consultation process but not the homeopathic remedy: a randomized controlled clinical trial. Rheumatology (Oxford). **50**(6), 1070–1082 (2011). doi:10.1093/rheumatology/keq234. Epub 13 Nov 2010

Campbell, A.: The origins of classical homoeopathy? Complement Ther. Med. **7**(2), 76–82 (1999)

Campbell, A.: The origins of classical homoeopathy. Complement Ther. Med. **7**(2), 76–82 (1999)

Campbell, A.: Homeopathy in Perspective. Lulu Enterprises, London (2014)

Chatwin, J.: Damning with faint praise: how homoeopaths talk about conventional medicine with their patients. Commun. Med. **9**(3), 191–201 (2012)

Chikramane, P.S., Suresh, A.K., Bellare, J.R., Kane, S.G.: Extreme homeopathic dilutions retain starting materials: a nanoparticulate perspective. Homeopathy **99**(4), 231–242 (2010). doi:10.1016/j.homp.2010.05.006

Cohen, M.H.: Legal ramifications of homeopathy. J. Altern. Complement Med. **1**(4), 393–398 (1995)

Csupor, D., Boros, K., Hohmann, J.: Low potency homeopathic remedies and allopathic herbal medicines: is there an overlap. PLoS One **8**(9), e74181 (2013). doi:10.1371/journal.pone.0074181. 3 Sep 2013. eCollection 2013

Dantas, F., Rampes, H.: Do homeopathic medicines provoke adverse effects? A systematic review. Br. Homeopath. J. **89**(Suppl 1), S35–S38 (2000)

Davidson, J.: A Century of Homeopaths: Their Influence on Medicine and Health. Springer, New York (2014)

Dean, M.E.: A homeopathic origin for placebo controls: 'an invaluable gift of God'. Altern. Ther. Health Med. **6**(2), 58–66 (2000)

Drewsen, S.: Hahnemanns Streit mit der "bisherigen alten Arzneischule" als Streit um wissenschaftliche Methoden. Versuch einer Rekonstruktion und Würdigung seines Ansatzes zur

Grundlegung der Heilkunde als eines methodenkritischen Ansatzes. Wurzbg Medizinhist Mitt. **11**, 45–58 (1993)

Ernst, E.: 'Neue Deutsche Heilkunde': complementary/alternative medicine in the Third Reich. Complement Ther. Med. **9**(1), 49–51 (2001)

Ernst, E.: A systematic review of systematic reviews of homeopathy. Br. J. Clin. Pharmacol. **54**(6), 577–582 (2002)

Ernst, E.: The benefits of Arnica: 16 case reports. Homeopathy **92**(4), 217–219 (2003)

Ernst, E.: Homoeopathy and I. Int. J. Clin. Pract. **63**(11), 1558–1561 (2009). doi:10.1111/j.1742-1241.2009.02169.x

Ernst, E.: Homeopathy: what does the "best" evidence tell us. Med. J. Aust. **192**(8), 458–460 (2010a)

Ernst, E.: The ethics of British professional homoeopaths. Int. J. Clin. Pract. **64**(2), 147–148 (2010b). doi:10.1111/j.1742-1241.2009.02249.x. Epub 3 Nov 2009

Ernst, E., Hung, S.K.: Great expectations: what do patients using complementary and alternative medicine hope for? Patient **4**(2), 89–101 (2011). doi:10.2165/11586490-000000000-00000

Ernst, E., Kaptchuk, T.J.: Homeopathy revisited. Arch. Intern. Med. **156**(19), 2162–2164 (1996)

Eyles, C., Leydon, G.M., Brien, S.B.: Forming connections in the homeopathic consultation. Patient Educ. Couns. **89**(3), 501–506 (2012). doi:10.1016/j.pec.2012.02.004. Epub 26 Feb 2012

Fisher, P.: What is homeopathy? An introduction. Front. Biosci. (Elite Ed.) **1**(4), 1669–1682 (2012)

Freckelton, I.: Death by homeopathy: issues for civil, criminal and coronial law and for health service policy. J. Law. Med. **19**(3), 454–478 (2012)

Furnham, A.: Ignorance about homeopathy. J. Altern. Complement Med. **5**(5), 475–478 (1999)

Furnham, A., Smith, C.: Choosing alternative medicine: a comparison of the beliefs of patients visiting a general practitioner and a homoeopath. Soc. Sci. Med. **26**(7), 685–689 (1988)

Gantenbein, U.L.: The First School of Vienna and Samuel Hahnemann's pharmaceutical techniques. Med. Ges. Gesch. **19**, 229–249 (2000)

Gemmell, D.M.: Everyday Homoeopathy (The Beaconsfield homoeopathic library). Beaconsfield Publishers Ltd, Beaconsfield (1997)

Ghosh, A.K.: A short history of the development of homeopathy in India. Homeopathy **99**(2), 130–136 (2010). doi:10.1016/j.homp.2009.10.001

Grabia, S., Ernst, E.: Homeopathic aggravations: a systematic review of randomised, placebo-controlled clinical trials. Homeopathy **92**(2), 92–98 (2003)

Gunther, M.: The homeopathic patient: comparative results of homeopathic and conventional GP patient interviews. Med. Ges. Gesch. **18**, 119–136 (1999)

Hahnemann, S.: The Chronic Diseases; Their Specific Nature and Homoeopathic Treatment. Boericke & Tafel, Philadelphia (1896)

Hahnemann, S.: In: Hughes, R. (ed.) Materia Medica Pura (translated by Dudgeon, R.E.), vol. II. B Jain Publishers Pvt Ltd, Noida (2003)

Hahnemann, S.: Organon of the Rational Art of Healing. Everyman's Library No. 663. Oxford University Press, Oxford (2010)

Handley, R.: In Search of the Later Hahnemann (Beaconsfield Homoeopathic Library). Beaconsfield Publishers Ltd, Beaconsfield (1997)

Homöopathie - König, Peter (Hg.): Durch Ähnliches heilen. Homöopathie in Österreich, Orac Verlag, Vienna (1996)

Jargin, S.V.: Hormesis and homeopathy: the artificial twins. J. Intercult. Ethnopharmacol. **4**(1), 74–77 (2015). doi:10.5455/jice.20140929114417. Epub 28 Nov 2014

Jonas, W.B., Kaptchuk, T.J., Linde, K.: A critical overview of homeopathy. Ann. Intern. Med. **138**(5), 393–399 (2003)

Jütte, R.: Hahnemann and placebo. Homeopathy **103**(3), 208–212 (2014). doi:10.1016/j.homp.2014.03.003. Epub 13 Apr 2014

Jütte, R., Riley, D.: A review of the use and role of low potencies in homeopathy. Complement Ther. Med. **13**(4), 291–296 (2005). Epub 16 Nov 2005

Kaiser, W., Völker, A.: Ars medica Anhaltina (III): the Anhalt Hahnemann interpretation and the Köthen Homeopathic Institute. Z. Gesamte Inn. Med. **41**(12), 348–355 (1986)

Kaplan, B.: Homoeopathy: 3. Everyday uses for all the family. Prof. Care Mother Child. **4**(7), 212–213 (1994)

Karrasch, B.: Die hompathische Laienbewegung in Deutschland zwischen 1933 und 1945. Med. Ges. Gesch. **15**, 167–194 (1996)

Kenny, M.G.: A darker shade of green: medical botany, homeopathy, and cultural politics in interwar Germany. Soc. Hist. Med. **15**(3), 481–504 (2002)

Kóczián, M., Kölnei, L.: History of homeopathy in Hungary 1820–1990. Orvostort. Kozl. **47**(1–4), 75–110 (2002)

Lang, C.J.: The four medical theses of Samuel Hahnemann (1755–1843). J. Med. Biogr. **24**(2), 243–252 (2016). doi:10.1177/0967772014526347. Epub 27 Mar 2014

Leary, B.: The homoepathic management of cholera in the nineteenty century with special reference to the epidemic in London, 1854. Med. Ges. Gesch. **16**, 125–144 (1997)

Leary, B.: The early work of Dr. Edward Bach. Br. Homeopath. J. **88**(1), 28–30 (1999)

Lewith, G.T., Kenyon, J.N., Broomfield, J., Prescott, P., Goddard, J., Holgate, S.T.: Is electrodermal testing as effective as skin prick tests for diagnosing allergies? A double blind, randomised block design study. BMJ **322**(7279), 131–134 (2001). 20 Jan 2001

Linde, K., Clausius, N., Ramirez, G., Melchart, D., Eitel, F., Hedges, L.V., Jonas, W.B.: Are the clinical effects of homeopathy placebo effects? A meta-analysis of placebo-controlled trials. Lancet **350**(9081), 834–843 (1997). 20 Sept 1997. Erratum in Lancet **351**(9097), 220, 17 Jan 1998

Linde, K., Scholz, M., Ramirez, G., Clausius, N., Melchart, D., Jonas, W.B.: Impact of study quality on outcome in placebo-controlled trials of homeopathy. J. Clin. Epidemiol. **52**(7), 631–636 (1999)

Linde, K., Jonas, W.B., Melchart, D., Willich, S.: The methodological quality of randomized controlled trials of homeopathy, herbal medicines and acupuncture. Int. J. Epidemiol. **30**(3), 526–531 (2001)

Livingston, R.: Homoeopathy: Evergreen Medicine - Jewel in the Medical Crown. Asher and Asher, Poole (1993)

Mathie, R.T., Clausen, J.: Veterinary homeopathy: systematic review of medical conditions studied by randomised trials controlled by other than placebo. BMC Vet. Res. **15**(11), 236 (2015a). doi:10.1186/s12917-015-0542-2

Mathie, R.T., Clausen, J.: Veterinary homeopathy: meta-analysis of randomised placebo-controlled trials. Homeopathy **104**(1), 3–8 (2015b). doi:10.1016/j.homp.2014.11.001. Epub 17 Dec 2014

Mathie, R.T., Lloyd, S.M., Legg, L.A., Clausen, J., Moss, S., Davidson, J.R., Ford, I.: Randomised placebo-controlled trials of individualised homeopathic treatment: systematic review and meta-analysis. Syst. Rev. **6**(3), 142 (2014). doi:10.1186/2046-4053-3-142

McCarney, R., Fisher, P., Spink, F., Flint, G., van Haselen, R.: Can homeopaths detect homeopathic medicines by dowsing? A randomized, double-blind, placebo-controlled trial. J. R. Soc. Med. **95**(4), 189–191 (2002)

Moffett, J.R.: Miasmas, germs, homeopathy and hormesis: commentary on the relationship between homeopathy and hormesis. Hum. Exp. Toxicol. **29**(7), 539–543 (2010). doi:10.1177/0960327110369855

Mudry, A.: Is homeopathy a scientific therapy? Rev. Med. Suisse Romande. **120**(2), 171–177 (2000)

Ostermann, J.K., Reinhold, T., Witt, C.M.: PLoS One **10**(7), e0134657 (2015a). doi:10.1371/journal.pone.0134657. eCollection 2015. 31 July 2015. Can Additional Homeopathic Treatment Save Costs? A Retrospective Cost-Analysis Based on 44500 Insured Persons

Ostermann, J.K., Reinhold, T., Witt, C.M.: Can additional homeopathic treatment save costs? A retrospective cost-analysis based on 44500 insured persons. PLoS One **10**(7), e0134657 (2015b). doi:10.1371/journal.pone.0134657. 31 July 2015. eCollection 2015

Pinet, P.: Hufeland (1762–1836) and homeopathy. Rev. Hist. Pharm. (Paris) **50**(335), 481–494 (2002)

Pinet, P.: Alchemy, freemasonry and homeopathy. Rev. Hist. Pharm. (Paris) **59**(370), 175–192 (2011)

Pinet, P.: Alchemy, freemasonry and homeopathy. Rev. Hist. Pharm. (Paris) **59**(370), 175–192 (2011)

Piolot, M., Fagot, J.P., Rivière, S., Fagot-Campagna, A., Debeugny, G., Couzigou, P., Alla, F.: Homeopathy in France in 2011–2012 according to reimbursements in the French national health insurance database (SNIIRAM). Fam. Pract. **32**(4), 442–448 (2015). doi:10.1093/fampra/cmv028. Epub 28 Apr 2015

Posadzki, P., Alotaibi, A., Ernst, E.: Adverse effects of homeopathy: a systematic review of published case reports and case series. Int. J. Clin. Pract. **66**(12), 1178–1188 (2012). doi:10.1111/ijcp.12026

Ransom, S.: Homoeopathy PB: What Are We Swallowing?. John Ritchie Ltd, Kilmarnock (2000)

Rásky, E., Freidl, W., Haidvogl, M., Stronegger, W.J.: Work and life style of homeopathic physicians in Austria. A descriptive study. Wien Med. Wochenschr. **144**(17), 419–424 (1994)

Reichenbach, K.R., Friedrich, C.: Charles-Gaspard Peschier (1782–1853), a pioneer of homeopathic medicine in Franco-phone areas. Med. Ges. Gesch. **21**, 143–172 (2002)

Richard Haehl, M.D.: Samuel Hahnemann: His Life & Work. Forgotten Books, London (2012)

Rieder, M.J., Robinson, J.L.: 'Nosodes' are no substitute for vaccines. Paediatr. Child. Health. **20**(4), 219–222 (2015)

Rizza, E.: Samuel Hahnemann: a mystical empiricist. A study of the origin and development of the homeopathic medical system. Med. Secoli. **6**(3), 515–524 (1994)

Schmacke, N., Müller, V., Stamer, M.: What is it about homeopathy that patients value? and what can family medicine learn from this. Qual. Prim. Care **22**(1), 17–24 (2014)

Schmidt, J.M.: The development of homeopathy in the United States. Gesnerus **51**(Pt 1–2), 84–100 (1994)

Schmidt, J.M.: Samuel Hahnemann and the principle of similars. Med. Ges. Gesch. **29**, 151–184 (2010a)

Schmidt, J.M.: The concept of health - in the history of medicine and in the writings of Hahnemann. Homeopathy **99**(3), 215–220 (2010b). doi:10.1016/j.homp.2010.05.004

Schmidt, J.M.: 200 years organon of medicine - a comparative review of its six editions (1810–1842). Homeopathy **99**(4), 271–277 (2010c). doi:10.1016/j.homp.2010.08.004

Shang, A., Huwiler-Müntener, K., Nartey, L., Jüni, P., Dörig, S., Sterne, J.A., Pewsner, D., Egger, M.: Are the clinical effects of homoeopathy placebo effects? Comparative study of placebo-controlled trials of homoeopathy and allopathy. Lancet **366**(9487), 726–732 (2005). 27 Aug–2 Sep 2005

Smith, K.: Against homeopathy-a utilitarian perspective. Bioethics **26**(8), 398–409 (2012). doi:10.1111/j.1467-8519.2010.01876.x. Epub 14 Feb 2011

Stollberg, G.: Patients and homeopathy: an overview of sociological literature. Med. Ges. Gesch. **18**, 103–118 (1999)

Swayne, J.: International Dictionary of Homeopathy. Churchill Livingstone, London (2000)

Teixeira, M.Z.: Similitude in modern pharmacology. Br. Homeopath. J. **88**(3), 112–120 (1999)

Teixeira, J.: Can water possibly have a memory? A sceptical view. Homeopathy **96**(3), 158–162 (2007)

Thomas, P.: Homeopathy in the USA. Br. Homeopath. J. **90**(2), 99–103 (2001)

Thoms, U.: Homoeopathy, a contentious issue: clinical experiments to support homeopathy in the military and in the Berlin Charité, 1820–1840. Med. Ges. Gesch. **21**, 173–218 (2002)

Trépardoux, F.: Prosecution of Mélanie Hahnemann in 1847 at the court of Paris: illegal practise of pharmacy and medicine. Rev. Hist. Pharm. (Paris) **50**(335), 427–438 (2002)

Ullman, D.: The Homeopathic Revolution: Why Famous People and Cultural Heroes Choose Homeopathy. North Atlantic Books, Berkeley (2007)

van Haselen, R.A.: The relationship between homeopathy and the Dr Bach system of flower remedies: a critical appraisal. Br. Homeopath. J. **88**(3), 121–127 (1999)

Vickers, A.J.: Independent replication of pre-clinical research in homeopathy: a systematic review. Forsch. Komplementarmed. **6**(6), 311–320 (1999)

Vieracker, V.: Nosode and sarcode therapies and their history-a controversial inheritance. Med. Ges. Gesch. **33**, 155–177 (2015)

Viksveen, P., Dymitr, Z., Simoens, S.: Economic evaluations of homeopathy: a review. Eur. J. Health. Econ. **15**(2), 157–174 (2014). doi:10.1007/s10198-013-0462-7. Epub 10 Feb 2013

Vithoulkas, G.: Homoeopathy: past, present and future. Br. J. Clin. Pharmacol. **45**(6), 613 (1998)

Vockeroth, W.G.: Veterinary homeopathy: an overview. Can. Vet. J. **40**(8), 592–594 (1999)

von Ammon, K., Frei-Erb, M., Cardini, F., Daig, U., Dragan, S., Hegyi, G., Roberti di Sarsina, P., Sörensen, J., Lewith, G.: Complementary and alternative medicine provision in Europe-first results approaching reality in an unclear field of practices. Forsch. Komplementmed. **19**(Suppl 2), 37–43 (2012). doi:10.1159/000343129

Werner, P.: Zu den Auseinandersetzungen um die Institutionalisierung von Naturheilkunde und Homöopathie an der Friedrich-Wilhelms-Universität zu Berlin zwischen 1919 und 1933. Med. Ges. Gesch. **12**, 205–219 (1993)

Weymayr, C.: Scientability - a concept for the handling of homeopathic remedies by EbM. Z. Evid. Fortbild. Qual. Gesundhwes. **107**(9–10), 606–610 (2013). doi:10.1016/j.zefq.2013.10.022. Epub 14 Nov 2013

Witt, C.M., Bluth, M., Albrecht, H., Weisshuhn, T.E., Baumgartner, S., Willich, S.N.: The in vitro evidence for an effect of high homeopathic potencies-a systematic review of the literature. Complement Ther. Med. **15**(2), 128–138 (2007). Epub 28 Mar 2007

Wootton, D.: Bad Medicine: Doctors Doing Harm Since Hippocrates. OUP, Oxford (2007)

Printed in the United States
By Bookmasters